Failure as a Path to Success
Embracing Setbacks As Learning Opportunities

By

Drew S. Baldridge

Copyright © 2023 by Drew S. Baldridge

All rights reserved. No part of this book may be reproduced, stored in a retrieval system, or transmitted in any form or by any means, electronic, mechanical, photocopying, recording, or otherwise, without the prior written permission of the author, except for brief quotations embodied in essential reviews and certain other noncommercial uses permitted by copyright law.

Disclaimer:

The information contained in this book, "Failure as a Path to Success: Embracing Setbacks As Learning Opportunities," is for general informational purposes only. The author, Drew S. Baldridge, makes no representations or warranties of any kind, express or implied, about the completeness, accuracy, reliability, suitability, or availability of the information contained herein. Any reliance you place on such information is strictly at your own risk.

The author is not a licensed professional, and the information provided in this book is not a substitute for professional advice. Readers are encouraged to seek professional guidance, as necessary, for their specific situations.

The author and publisher disclaim any liability for any loss or damage arising directly or indirectly from the use of this book. By reading this book, you agree to absolve the author and publisher from any and all liability.

While the author has made every effort to ensure that the information contained in this book is accurate and up-to-date, the rapidly changing nature of knowledge and the individual circumstances of each reader may necessitate modifications or updates to the content.

The views and opinions expressed in this book are those of the author and do not necessarily reflect the official policy or position of any organizations mentioned or referred to in the text.

Every effort has been made to trace and acknowledge copyright material used in this book. If any omissions or errors are brought to the attention of the author or publisher, they will be corrected in subsequent editions.

Your use of this book indicates your acceptance of these terms and conditions.

About the Author

Drew S. Baldridge is a committed and passionate independent writer whose goal is to produce content that promotes personal development and better living. Drew is a writer with a distinctive viewpoint on the path from failure to success. He is deeply committed to assisting people in overcoming challenges, embracing self-improvement, and realising the power of resilience.

Drew is a talented and adaptable writer who excels at making difficult concepts understandable and approachable. His writing appears in a variety of formats, including books, articles, blogs, and social media posts. One of Drew's best writing qualities is his ability to personally connect with readers, which makes his work interesting and approachable for readers of different backgrounds.

Drew's collection of work demonstrates his commitment to the idea of "Failure as a Path to Success". He encourages others to see setbacks as priceless teaching moments by drawing on his own experiences and observations. In addition to giving guidance, he shares in his writings the lessons he has discovered on his own path to both professional and personal growth.

Drew S. Baldridge's work is a great resource if you're looking for advice on conquering obstacles, navigating life's uncertainties, or just finding motivation to follow your own route to success. His writing demonstrates his dedication to assisting people in leading more fulfilled lives, making him a reliable resource for anybody looking for insight, inspiration, and a novel viewpoint on the path to personal growth.

Table of content

Introduction

We often find ourselves enthralled by the tales of those who have achieved the highest point in their ambitions since we live in a society that usually praises success and achievement. Their successes and victories, as well as the magnitude of their achievements, are proclaimed in the headlines. But what about the times that are hidden behind the blinding curtain of misfortune and struggle, moments that happen beneath those brilliant spotlights?

This book explores the unsaid truths, the seldom-told stories, and the unwritten chapters that offer a radically different viewpoint on the path to success. It is a challenge to venture into the unknown territory of failure—not as a destination, but rather as a necessary step on the way to success.

The book "Failure as a Path to Success: Embracing Setbacks and Learning Opportunities" serves as a guide through the rough waters of life. It is evidenced that success is often discovered in the midst of failure and in the lessons learnt when the journey takes an unexpected turn, rather than at some far-off summit.

Come along on an inspiring trip through the tales of people who overcame adversity by accepting their mistakes and using them as learning opportunities. Together, we'll uncover the compelling stories of fortitude, creativity, and personal development that surface when we decide to view failure as a chance rather than a barrier.

Welcome to a world where success is paved with the inspirational tales of people who dared to accept change.
Welcome to a world where, all along the route to success, one can find the inspirational tales of those who dared to accept their shortcomings and see the remarkable in the ordinary.

Chapter One: Failure as a Step Towards Success

Failure is success in progress!
On the path to success, failure is a necessary step in the process. One must learn from mistakes and overcome obstacles in order to succeed.
You might fail at times in your life, so it's essential to develop coping mechanisms and strategies to get past these obstacles. Even while it may seem like a bad experience, failure can also present a chance for improvement.
Finding constructive methods to accept setbacks and go forward after them can be facilitated by learning about failure and creating tactics for getting past it.
Unbelievably, there will always be failure in life.
Life occasionally knocks you down, but how you get back up is what counts.

The state of not achieving an objective or the desired result is called failure. Even though they are sometimes seen as the antithesis of success, daily life setbacks offer the most chances for personal development. Since failure and unconventional thinking can lead to creativity and learning, the most effective leaders support them.

Each has its own interpretation of what it means to be unsuccessful. It's not a single event, but a process. Whatever description it goes by, everyone will encounter it at some point in their lives. However, setbacks can pave the way for fresh achievements and triumphs.

We will all experience failure at some point in our life, and it will seem like the end of the world. Whatever your definition, it's something that we've all dealt with at some point and it's not something that's simple to move past. Failure can be a life-shaking experience if it transforms your life, destroys relationships, or depresses your career graph.

It isn't always easy to get back up, dust yourself off, and move on, but doing so is what gets you to the next big thing. Failure can take many different forms, such as losing a lucrative business transaction or failing a test.

The anguish always has the same shattering wavelength, even as the gain fluctuates. How quickly you succeed depends on how you chose to use the lessons you learn from your mistakes. Because of this, failing becomes the most valuable life lesson that you can get by forcing yourself to strive towards your objective.

There will always be obstacles in the way of your aim. Even if not every obstacle will lead to success, accepting failure as a necessary part of the process can inspire you to keep trying. Continue trying until you achieve your objective.

The proverb "If you have never failed, you have never lived" is used frequently. It's not surprising that a lot of people are reluctant to admit they've failed or to discuss it, but the reality is that everyone has failed and will fail again.
A successful person understands that every success story begins with failure. Failure teaches us more about ourselves and what we want out of life. Additionally, we gain more insight into what doesn't work for us or in our life, which enables us to make wiser choices for our next pursuits.

You learn what should work and what doesn't with every unsuccessful attempt. Never assume that someone's achievement is the result of pure luck. Many people simply pay attention to their achievements, ignoring the many years of hardship and setbacks they experienced.
Every setback identifies a mistake you could have prevented, a necessary practice, and a skill that needs honing. It's safer to suggest that failing serves as a springboard for achievement.

Many people work hard to achieve success because they believe that it is all that is necessary to have a meaningful existence. However, this is untrue! Being successful without ever failing will never suffice as sufficient training.

Because they have been able to overcome them and learn from them, successful people embrace their failures.
Even though it can be frightening, failure is a chance for us to develop and learn.
Failures frequently have reasons. It's crucial that you resist letting it defeat you.

Thus, don't be scared of failing. It's a necessary step on the path to success. Life's best teacher is failure. It humbles you and strengthens your character. Failure is success suspended until the proper time; in the meanwhile, you have to put in a lot of effort, think clearly, and act consistently.

How Progress Is Made by Failure

Failure frequently has a bitter and unappealing taste. We make every effort to avoid failing because we fear it. However, every successful individual has, in reality, traveled a long and worn path strewn with countless instances of failure along the way.

Seeing the less glamorous but equally important aspects of their journey that aren't being shared might be challenging when our social media feeds are filled with success and celebration stories.
Our conception of success needs to be revised.
Some excellent reasons why failure prepares us for success, even though it may not be an easy concept to accept.

1. The finest teacher is a failure.
It would be hard to determine what works and what doesn't if you were never unsuccessful. Similar to an experiment, failure teaches us what doesn't work in terms of success. It indicates that we were able to test our theories and determine whether or not they were sound. Having gone through this firsthand, you will be far more likely to remember the lessons you've learnt because the emotions that arise from failure can imprint the lesson in your mind.

2. Your potential is unleashed by failure.
You can feel the lowest when you fail. However, failure might inspire you to do things you've never considered if you can channel your displeasure into something positive. If you hadn't failed, this might have revealed latent potential that you were unaware of.

Failure might motivate you to use your other assets and innovative thinking, which are traits that can lead you to success.

3. Failure makes you more modest.
It's possible to become extremely proud of yourself if you've had multiple accomplishments or if you come from a wealthy background. It's equally crucial to believe in your own ability, but if you let pride get the better of you, it can lead to disaster. Failure serves as a helpful reminder that despite your accomplishments, you can always learn new things and do better. It's not about bowing your head in shame; it's just about remembering to glance occasionally behind and below your feet.

4. Failure presents opportunities.
It's been said that you can only fail completely when you give up. However, there is a proper time to give up and move on in other situations. And when you fail, it's one of the best markers for this. Failure may be the signal that you need to break free and have new dreams. And that fresh vision might hold the key to your long-awaited triumph.

5. Your mirror is a failure.
It's been said that you can learn a lot about
someone by seeing them at their lowest.
Your innate nature can be inferred from your
reaction and handling of failure. You might be
shocked to learn how high your failure threshold is.
Knowing that this might be one of your greatest
assets and what sets you apart from those who give
up easily is inspiring.
Furthermore, you may be able to strengthen your
resilience as a result of this experience, even if your
failure threshold is lower than you previously
believed.

6. Character is shaped by failure.
You might have wanted to give up completely after
your first setback. However, the pain will
progressively lessen after you fail multiple times.
You'll soon be able to maintain your composure
under pressure and develop an unwaveringly
optimistic outlook.
You can think more clearly and make better
decisions when you can learn to regulate your
emotions in difficult situations.

Thus, the next time you hear about someone's
achievement, try not to concentrate on that one

instance. Recognise that their success started much earlier—the 99 other times they failed but persisted. Success isn't just about winning; it's about experiencing highs and lows, and that's how it should be. That's when we actually start to grow and advance.

When we approach failure with a "no fear" perspective, we may take advantage of any potential action-outcome synergy. Instead of actively seeking out failure, you should embrace difficulties that don't always turn out well.

It's about discovering your own strength, whatever it may be and however it may be used, and about taking lessons from the blunders that resulted in an unsuccessful conclusion. Accept new directions and have an open mind to all of the options that are in front of you.

Failure helps you mentally get ready to overcome the obstacles that lie ahead and gets you ready for your next potential stumble. Failure forces you to operate in a realm you never knew existed; it's a transformative experience that makes you a better version of yourself.

Failing develops your strength, skill, empathy, compassion, and kindness. It also aids in changing the way you interact with other people.

Failure, in every sense, brings out the finest in human qualities before you achieve your pinnacle of achievement.

Benefits Of Failure
Although nobody likes to fail, there are a number of really significant advantages that come with it, which emphasizes how crucial it is to develop coping mechanisms.

You can learn from your mistakes.
Studies reveal that your brain enlarges during the process of organizing memories of an encounter. When you make mistakes, your brain builds new neural connections by assimilating fresh data and distilling the lessons learned from the mistakes made. Put another way, learning from mistakes profoundly changes and matures the brain.

A failure is an act of risk-taking.
You are probably not pushing yourself past your comfort zone if you are successful in all you do. By taking on risks and recognising that failure is a possibility, you may discover that you identify more creative solutions or greater successes.

Failure offers chances for quick development.
It is possible to progress quickly when you test theories, take advice from others, and learn from mistakes.
Let us examine why accepting such moments can truly be your greatest asset and show you that failure is not the end of the world.
Opportunities come into the world when you fail.

Failure offers an extremely special chance for personal development.
Rather than trying to respond to things that happened to you (such the things your parents usually talk about), you are more likely to inspire change by the way you choose to respond to your own failure.

While taking advice from others is a valuable resource, trying to model your success after theirs will only make failure much more excruciating.

Failure can sometimes present chances to see things differently.
Sometimes you have to fail miserably on the first attempt before realizing it's not the proper route for you. It's quite OK to look for the correct path.
Discovering your true passion in life can be facilitated by failure.

Failure is therefore the road to success.
A chance to assess and enhance your capabilities is presented by failure.
It doesn't follow that a skill you feel you have isn't a strength just because you don't succeed in it.
Perhaps you can identify the ideal approach to apply your strengths if you reassess and take a step back. Are you going to sit on the ground and forget who you are when you are knocked down, or are you going to rise back up and become stronger?
The choice is actually yours to take.

The stories of the world's most powerful and well-known individuals are ones of struggle and failure that honed them into the brilliant gems they are today.
Although the founder of social media, Mark Zuckerberg, is currently among the wealthiest and most successful people, his initial network, Facemash, was a huge failure that did not turn out well for him. In addition, Mark was sued; the case was eventually resolved for an astounding 1.2 million Facebook shares.

In order to keep unpleasant feelings like rage, shame, or worry from negatively impacting you and other people, it's essential to deal with failure.
These feelings have an impact on decisions and

relationships, which makes it difficult to move past setbacks and make progress. Try to change your perspective after a failure so that you can learn from it, prevent similar mistakes in the future, and accept that while failures are inevitable, they do not define you.

You can more effectively process and overcome the range of emotions that may accompany failure if you give it some thought and take some time to acknowledge and accept it.

You might fail at times in your life, so it's essential to develop coping mechanisms and strategies to get past these obstacles. Even while it may seem like a bad experience, failure can also present a chance for improvement. Finding constructive methods to accept setbacks and go forward after them can be facilitated by learning about failure and creating tactics for getting past it.

Achieving Success Beyond Rejection
Rejection is awful.
It aches.
Nobody enjoys being turned down. However, rejection offers you a chance to develop, learn, and advance in your quest for professional success.

"Success Beyond Rejection" refers to reaching your
objectives and aspirations in spite of obstacles or
rejection. It's about going after your goals without
letting "no" or failure deter you.
Rejection offers you an opportunity to develop and
learn, opening up new avenues for achievement.
Many prosperous people experienced rejection but
kept going anyhow, and their tenacity paid off in
the form of amazing achievements.
"Success Beyond Rejection" is therefore about
perseverance, self-belief, and pursuing your goals in
spite of obstacles.

Have no fear of failing.
The only way you fail is if you don't gain any
knowledge from the event.
Consider every setback as a chance to improve.

Fear is the adversary of confidence in oneself and of
a successful job. Most people are afraid of rejection,
criticism, and failure. It's just typical.
Everyone wants to feel confident about themselves.
Rejection, criticism, and failure are unpleasant
things to go through.
Because they make us feel horrible about ourselves
and diminish our self-worth, we frequently refrain
from taking risks that we fear may result in
rejection, failure, or criticism.

But in order to build the kind of life and professional success you deserve, you must have the guts to take risks that could lead to rejection, failure, or criticism.

Rejection, criticism, and failure provide you the chance to improve and flourish. Rejection, criticism, and failure are inevitabilities. Rejection, criticism, and failure are the results. They are the outcome of your actions. You are not like them. Everyone errs and fails occasionally.
Everyone has done something that makes someone else dislike or reject them. That does not imply that we are inadequate. It indicates that we have done some foolish things and made some bad decisions.

Rejection, criticism, and failure provide you the chance to start anew, perhaps a little wiser. According to a quote by Buckminster Fuller, "Everything humans have learned has come from experience with trial and error." Humans have only ever gained knowledge by error.

Should your fear of not succeeding, receiving negative feedback, and being rejected paralyze you to the point of not wanting to take calculated chances, you will never grow or reach any of your objectives.

When you make mistakes or when people reject or criticize you, try not to be too hard on yourself. The best career advice I can give you is to work hard at determining why you didn't succeed and then try something different.
The next time you make a mistake, receive criticism, or are turned down, try asking yourself these questions.

I failed; why?

Why was I rejected or criticized?

What actions of mine led to the rejection, criticism, or failure?

What could I have done differently to avoid the rejection, criticism, or failure?

What can I take away from this experience?

What will I do when I get around to doing it again?

By doing this, you'll be able to benefit from failure, criticism, and rejection.

It is understandable that failure, criticism, and rejection can be difficult to recognise as opportunities or benefits. But if you look closely enough, you can see it. But the first step is to act on your fear. You'll achieve more career success the less fear of failure you have.

Here, the common sense career mentor point is straightforward. Those who are successful have self-confidence. People who are confident face their anxieties and take action. They adhere to the suggestions released from their mistakes in life. "Don't let failure scare you. The only way you fail is if you don't gain any knowledge from the event.

Consider every setback as a chance to improve. The three things we dread most are rejection, criticism, and failure. Adhere to this career guidance. You may increase your confidence and success by making the decision to recognise and capitalize on the lessons that can be learned from your mistakes. It's unfortunate but true that achieving professional success frequently comes with a price: rejection, criticism, and failure.
Acting and overcoming your fear of rejection, criticism, and failure will have a significant positive impact on your life.

When you receive rejections,you may choose to
either accept them, reassess the concepts, make the
required adjustments, and look for other markets,
or you can become infuriated and take the rejection
personally.
We've all experienced rejection in some way,
whether it was from a broken relationship, a
professional concept that was turned down, getting
passed over for a promotion, or being left out of a
social invitation. Rejection or exclusion may be a
terrible sensation that, if not handled appropriately,
can drastically alter your outlook on life.

To begin, think on these essential components for
overcoming rejection:
1 .Recognise Your Feelings
When rejection occurs, it hurts, and you should not
try to suppress your feelings of rage, frustration, or
despair. In actuality, suppressing these feelings can
lead to resentment and make it more difficult to
move past rejection.
You should definitely take a step back and address
your feelings if you find yourself blaming someone
else for hurting you, the fact that you weren't
chosen, or the injustice of life to others on a regular
basis.

Start by recording in a personal notebook the reasons for your anger, the hurt you experience, and how much you object to what transpired. Although acknowledging your emotions is a positive thing, try not to let them control your decisions or your ideas. It is possible to get over the uncomfortable emotions. Concentrate on all of your blessings.

Recall the occasions when you achieved success or were selected for leadership roles. Although being rejected doesn't mean you won't get another chance, you run the risk of turning into the kind of poisonous person that nobody wants to be around if you let yourself become fixated on what went wrong and practice your angry response. Being rejected does not guarantee that you won't be given another chance.

Accept Restrictions

Although none of us like to admit it, we are all fallible. We each possess unique abilities, talents, and qualities. We wouldn't require the assistance of others if we could accomplish everything perfectly. Despite what the world frequently tells us, we were not created to be all-knowing and all-powerful. Recognising our shortcomings keeps us sincere and modest.

Recognise That Others Are Eligible
The fact that certain people are picked doesn't
imply that the others aren't deserving. Maybe you
have a less obvious career, position, or talent that
fits your personality and set of abilities perfectly.
Individuals relate to a variety of personality types,
and you might influence others more than people in
the spotlight with your understated example. You
might be able to help more people and engage with
them than a well-known person. It takes a certain
level of maturity to be able to celebrate others in
places you aspired to, but strive to overcome envy,
find contentment in your current situation, and
keep an eye out for new prospects.

Prepare for Ego
For most of us, ego is a major issue since we enjoy
the sensations of acceptance and acknowledgement.
Although the need for attention is innate in human
nature, this does not imply you have to limit
yourself to what you believe you deserve. God might
let specific experiences shape your spirituality or
teach you humility. Or perhaps you're in a waiting
phase while you build up your skill set and get
ready for what's to come.

Examine Rejection with a Broad Lens
Everyone has experienced rejection at some point, but you don't have to let it define who you are and how you behave and respond going forward. Rejections are minor blips on the life radar, despite the fact that they feel significant at the moment. Acquire a broad perspective, acknowledging that everyone goes through periods of highs and lows.

After being rejected, don't write yourself off as a failure and only put forth a mediocre effort. Continue moving forward and don't let the past get in the way of your expectations for the future. Keep working as hard as you can for the sake of only one audience.

When you experience failure, try to do the following:
i) Return to your regular schedule;
 ii) Acknowledge that failure is a part of life and move on; and
iii) Learn from your mistakes.

What not to do in the event of failure:
i) Give up and quit trying
ii) Vary from your routine
iii) Give in to thoughts of inadequacy

How People's Views About Society Can Affect How They Respond To Failure.

Anybody can occasionally fail or make mistakes. Human history has frequently been founded on false beliefs, unclear viewpoints, and incorrect presumptions. Even successful people have false perceptions and bad experiences. However, they make the most of their circumstances—the awful things that happen to them and the sad events—and apply the lessons they learn to innovate and further their achievement.

There are several ways that society can affect how we view success or failure, including:

Cultural customs and principles: Different cultures may have different conceptions of what success or failure looks like, and these norms and values can affect how we view what is significant and what is not.

Media and advertising: These two sources can instill pressure to live up to predetermined ideals of status, money, and beauty as well as inaccurate expectations about what success looks like.

Education system: Our understanding of what it means to be successful might be influenced by how the system defines and measures success.

Social class: A person's socioeconomic background and social class can affect the opportunities and resources that are accessible to them, which in turn can affect how successful or unsuccessful they perceive themselves to be.

Peer pressure: By putting pressure on us to live up to particular standards and norms, peers and social groups can affect how we view success and failure. Political and economic systems: People's perceptions of success and failure can be influenced by the resources and opportunities that are made accessible to them by the political and economic systems in place.

Personal values and beliefs: These can influence how we define success and failure in our lives. It's essential to remember that our perceptions of success and failure are subject to many influences and are not necessarily grounded in objective reality. It's also essential to maintain a balanced viewpoint and avoid comparing oneself to others.

Your perception of failure has the power to either make you excel and achieve great success, or it can make you believe horrible things about people and yourself.

Types of Failure Perceptions
The idea of failing can either make you think bad things about other people and yourself, or it can inspire you to do well and achieve great achievement.

1.Those who believe failure is undesirable. Failure is absolute for them. Their behavior has a general inclination towards it. They are likely to think they are bad at everything if they "suck" at something. It's the mindset of "I'm a loser."
Their self-esteem is eroded by failure. Shameful about it, they feel certain they are incapable of greatness.
For them, failure is universal. Not wanting to be alone in their suffering, people often believe that everything in the world is horrible and in pain.
To them it is filled with bad people and only the smartest or strongest will survive.
Failure is inevitable when one has this thinking. Anyone will experience it; it's unavoidable and inescapable (particularly them).

As a result, you cannot learn from failure. It cannot help you grow. It loses significance. All you need to do is conceal it from others and from your resume. Their entire belief instills fear in them. They make every effort to succeed, even if it means missing out on life's great adventure.

Their greatest justification is failure. Their lack of effort stems from their failure. Rather than strive and daring to fail, they would prefer to have no idea what they could accomplish.

2. People who are successful also have to deal with failure. But they have distinct perspectives. It's part of the journey for them to fail.

Failure is relative to them. It relates to a specific item at a certain moment. It doesn't mean they're all awful people. Failure is personal as well. It's about them, and them alone. They don't attempt to assign blame on others for their own errors. They do not downplay their fear, failure, or responsibilities. To succeed, they make use of it and go beyond it.

In this way, failure can be adjusted. It implies that if they make a mistake once, it won't always happen again. Thus, they can construct tomorrow's success from today's failure.

Failure is an extremely effective teaching tool. When a youngster first learns to walk, they fall and then they get back up. Failure is a great tool for those who succeed. Their habit is to use it. They subdue it and make use of it as a springboard for their accomplishment. It serves as an experience badge.

It all boils down to evolution when you stop to think about it. Evolution indicates that we must be able to adapt. Humans would already be extinct if we weren't able to adapt to changes. It takes skill to deal with setbacks and seize opportunities when adapting.

People who are successful use failure as fuel. It's the enthusiasm they have when they realize they are almost there. When they accomplish something important, it's the power that motivates them. It's the fervor they feel when they realize they are almost there.

Advice on Handling Failure

1. Remain upbeat at all times. Your ability to bounce back from setbacks depends on your mental health. It's time to accept your defeat and move on; now is not the time to whine about the regulations and other things that went wrong for you.
Only those who have experienced failure themselves are able to muster the extra drive needed to prevail. Every real winner has experienced defeat at some point in their lives. You must continue to be resilient and optimistic about the future. Your response to failure, in my opinion, will determine whether you succeed or fail in life.

2. Show gratitude to others in your vicinity. This is the moment to thank your team if you have worked with one. Make sure they realize that you win and lose together as a team. Your group requires you. Don't blame anyone; this is simply a momentary setback, and you will still need them in the long term. Rearranging certain elements, such as your team, may be necessary to overcome a setback, but you must do it without undermining their confidence.

3. Examine the circumstances. Examine the situation closely. You have two options: either handle this alone or seek out a professional who can assist you in closely examining the circumstances and pointing out errors to ensure that the failure doesn't happen again. Whether it occurs in your personal or professional life, you must give issues careful thought.

Even though some of the largest brands have failed, they were unable to let it get to them or alter their business strategies. Those brands needed to properly analyze the situation and draw conclusions. Failing at something is preferable to trying nothing at all. Likewise, the majority of prosperous businesspeople are also specialists at failure. They've encountered multiple setbacks. Although all you could see is their achievements, remember that they likely had goals missed, time wasted etc.

4. Recognise your errors. You can learn how to prevent the mistakes you made in the future by being aware of them. As soon as you recognise your errors, make a real effort to prevent or correct them. You will never try something new if you are frightened of making mistakes.

5. Plan and give it another go. The winning spirit is the will to never give up. Attempt again and again until you succeed. You improve each time you attempt. Even though it might not be apparent right away, you are improving your abilities and methods for finishing the task. Thomas Edison advises us to keep trying and never give up. The quote, "I have not failed 10,000 times—I have successfully discovered 10,000 ways that will not work," is widely attributed to him.

Here are some more strategies to help you overcome failure:
Consider the potential for learning.
Not only may we learn from our mistakes to prevent repeating them, but we can also realize the value of failing by doing so. Maybe you discovered that you need to work on your communication abilities, or maybe you decided you weren't cut out for the position. Failures can give you insight into where you can make improvements, which enables you to come up with fresh ideas for personal development.

Draw inspiration from your errors.
You can learn from your mistakes and use them as motivation to make other positive changes in your life. For instance, if you erred, you might take the chance to devise a fresh approach to completing the

assignment or advancing the original objective. It might be beneficial to learn from your mistakes and use them as a springboard for creativity and problem-solving.

Adjust to evolving situations
When you stick to a pattern, it's easy to forget little things. For instance, if your work involves repetitive duties, you can fail to notice a small detail or to include a current update. When your routine shifts, it's crucial to give yourself more time to adjust. You might also decide to sometimes alter your schedule in order to sharpen your focus or attempt chores in a different approach that might stimulate originality and creative thinking.

Get a fresh viewpoint.
When you fail, see it as a chance to see things from a different angle. You might discover fresh perspectives on your routines by embracing your emotions, taking care of yourself, and reviewing your actions. Failure can be a terrific way to assess your habits and thought processes and come up with fresh approaches to problems or objectives. You could come up with different answers when you approach problems or objectives from a different angle.

Recognise when to move forward.
Taking stock of your mistakes might assist you in determining when to move on from a work or objective. It can be beneficial to admit when a goal is out of reach or doesn't meet your needs and expectations.

Your attention may be better directed towards other priorities that may better serve your long-term goals if you are able to let go of unattainable or superfluous aspirations through failure. For instance, if you're having trouble getting promoted at your current job, you can search for other options that better suit your requirements, goals, and skill set.

Chapter Two: The Failure Learning Curve

We may learn a great deal from nature, as it teaches us things in its own unique way. Consider yourself observing a plant's growth. It's like a little seed planted in the earth at first, with little visible development. However, with time, the plant begins to grow—little by little—and finally it develops into a large, lovely flower or a towering tree.

It's kind of like the learning curve in nature. It tells us that some things require patience and time to improve. As a plant grows slowly, so too do we learn and get better with time. Therefore, bear in mind that, like nature, it's acceptable to start small and keep expanding when you're attempting to get great at something.

Failure is frequently a potent driver for growth and learning. Errors and disappointments can teach us important lessons that help us succeed in the future.

Failing and being disappointed is one of the best ways to learn. God never promised an easy life, and it is never so. Disappointments and failures are life's learning curves. You are not a failure just because you failed at anything. Many would argue that it is preferable to take lessons from other people's mistakes. Even though it is undeniably true, experience is still the best teacher.

When we attempt something new or challenging, we may not always succeed the first time. You're okay! It somewhat resembles playing a video game. You might fail a level, but you keep trying rather than giving up.
You gain a little more knowledge on how to improve with each attempt. Thus, learning from failure entails utilizing your errors as teaching moments to improve your performance in the endeavor. It's like having a superpower that keeps getting better!

Failing is acceptable as long as you don't stay a failure. Refusing to try for success is staying a failure. Never give up on your quest for achievement, no matter how many times you fall short of your goals. But the secret to success in all such endeavors is to learn from your mistakes. You won't stop failing at everything if you don't learn from it. To achieve success, one must internalize the lessons learned from failure.

Failure teaches you what went wrong so that you don't make the same mistake(s) twice. It enables you to use more effective tactics, gain a better understanding of your past mistakes, etc.
Have you experienced failure in your profession, relationships, business, or other areas?
Apply the knowledge you get from these kinds of encounters to your future endeavors. Recall that life's disappointments serve as teaching opportunities. Use the knowledge you gain from them to attain the success you so desire.

Recognising initial failure and making course corrections based on what was learned is the healthiest response. Although reinterpreting failure as a teaching opportunity facilitates a swift turn around, the same failure is frequently repeated. For most lessons, learning is not a "once and done" process. Learning and failure are usually on a scale, not a binary relationship.
From a consequence standpoint, the pain will sound less intense if it is addressed as soon as it starts to ache. Everyone wants to learn things fast and painlessly, but some lessons are, in fact, best learnt only after suffering serious repercussions. These are undoubtedly the most important ones.

Failure of major consequence is the hardest to acknowledge, yet it's frequently essential to a leader's development.

Occasionally people repeat mistakes due to deeply rooted habits or beliefs; nevertheless, if a leader promptly owns up to their mistakes, they can make necessary corrections.

An essential first step towards success in any or all of our journeys is failure at first.

Life will inevitably involve failure. Everybody has encountered it at some point in their lives.

On the other hand, our success is determined by how we respond to failure.

Using Failure and Mistakes as Teaching Opportunities:

1. Establish a wall of failure: Keep a record of all your attempts that haven't paid off or produced the desired outcomes.

Perhaps the financing for your project was withheld, an interview went poorly, you didn't get the promotion, a presentation wasn't well received, or you weren't given the money you needed. Even though these may be unpleasant experiences, you will be able to recognise your efforts when you consider the work you have done.

A project that fails in one area can succeed in another down the road. You'll be able to see errors and difficulties as a necessary part of the process of producing successful results if you keep track of the number of failures required to achieve success.

2. Ditch the terminology of "win-lose": We frequently perceive life's experiences as binary, with winners and losers representing the two extremes of the spectrum. However, this isn't necessarily accurate to reality.
What if, in the process of winning a project, you end up losing a relationship? What happens if you don't win a client pitch, but you gain so much knowledge that you can use it in future pitches?
Instead of concentrating on success or victory as a result, change your perspective to appreciate the journey that brought you here as well as the drive, initiative, effort, and resourcefulness you displayed. You can find benefits in any circumstance, even when there are negative aspects, if you can learn to appreciate the process more than the result.

3. Admit your mistakes in real time: Looking back, you may be able to see how mistakes ultimately aided your professional development. Maybe you gained some valuable insight into what to do or even what not to do. Perhaps you developed

resilience, innovated, made a direction shift, or increased your motivation. Maybe you let go of something that you found to be unsatisfactory. While telling these stories as they happen makes a difference, they are still fantastic to share.
You can get support and lessen others' feelings of shame or embarrassment when they make errors if you can confide in people you trust about your experiences at that time.

In general, you should be proud of your mistakes if they demonstrate that you made a change. It is not helpful to go forward by maintaining toxic positivity and feigning happiness in the face of difficulty or severe disappointment; in the long run, this can be detrimental to one's mental health.
It's feasible to feel difficult emotions and still find strategies to go forward while also acknowledging and accepting the unpleasant sensations that come with failure.

The goal of failing forward is to get knowledge from the experience so that you can advance and improve yourself later on.
Not every failure results in future success; some errors serve as reminders of what we don't want or the improper way to handle a circumstance. But whenever things go wrong, there's always

something you can learn about the circumstance or yourself.

Key Reasons Failure Is A Part Of Success
You haven't learned if you haven't failed. The key to failure is to keep trying things you're not yet good at. Sure, sometimes we do well on our first attempt. Some people associate failure with shame, which causes them to experience crippling fear that prevents them from trying again. But for those who are dedicated to lifelong learning, failure is a driving force that encourages them to learn important lessons from their mistakes, keep going with greater grit, and pursue achievement using novel and creative methods.

The goal of failing forward is to gain knowledge from the event. It is important to acknowledge that not all setbacks result in success in the future, but even when things don't go as planned, you may always learn something.

First on Forbes' list of the world's wealthiest individuals, Jeff Bezos transformed Amazon from an online bookseller in 1994 to a major player in e-commerce today. But Bezos lost over a billion dollars in his first years of operation.

He learned from them and altered his direction rather than allowing them to discourage him and his vision. This is evident from many of his comments and deeds, which reflect the importance he places on lifelong learning and the ability to learn from mistakes in order to adapt and advance.

Any form of growth involves pushing boundaries and venturing into unknown areas. You won't always succeed in accomplishing your goals straight away when you take on new problems, try to come up with fresh solutions, or concentrate on deepening your understanding; in fact, you could feel as though you've failed, which can be unsettling to go through.

You can take advantage of mistakes, failure, and obstacles by changing your perspective to see them as steps towards achieving a successful and constructive outcome. If you concentrate on the benefits you stand to gain—such as increasing your knowledge base, honing your craft, or furthering your career or personal growth—this may seem less difficult. Sometimes learning new things and conquering obstacles will go well, and other times there can be hiccups.

As you begin to explore new ideas and exercise newly gained abilities, it's important to prepare yourself for future problems and acknowledge that failure is a typical part of the learning process.

It's imperative that we learn to fail in the workplace or our life pursuits both now and in the future. This may mean that people must learn to fail, make mistakes, and grapple with the complexity of new challenges without becoming overwhelmed or ashamed.
This can be facilitated by treating new endeavors like experiments, where there is no right or wrong answer, but different strategies can be tried and results can be evaluated in relation to objectives.

Instead of allowing failure to hold us back, we must learn how to harness it and turn it to our benefit. Reducing the stigma associated with failure and shifting attention to the final result is crucial to this. Avoid taking chances or attempting a different strategy because people are frequently afraid of things not working out because of the ensuing feelings of humiliation, embarrassment, and guilt.

To truly embrace and rejoice in failure, you must cultivate cognitive flexibility—reinterpreting trying circumstances, ideas, and feelings to see them as valuable aspects of life and work.

People who use failure as fuel for success recognise that opportunities and challenges will inevitably arise; failing at something need not be a bad thing; rather, it may indicate that you should try something different, keep honing a skill, or take a different path. You can start to view your failures as not failures at all, but rather an integral part of the process that is necessary for you to be able to advance in your profession, once you recognise that the majority of triumphs are built on the experience of numerous failures.

The good news is that you can use setbacks, obstacles, and blunders to your benefit. It all comes down to changing your viewpoint such that unplanned events are seen as a necessary component of growth and learning.
The secret is to get ready for whatever obstacles you may face and acknowledge that you might make mistakes when attempting to apply new concepts and abilities. It's also important for you to realize that making poor decisions is a common occurrence throughout the process.

In fact, if you can learn to embrace failure instead of merely accepting that mistakes will happen, you'll develop a mindset that will enable you to succeed.

Failure and setbacks can undermine your drive and self-worth, but they can also provide you with new perspectives and insights that will motivate you to fail your way to success.
Making mistakes along the route to success entails applying the knowledge you've gained from them to your desired outcomes.
You may fail if you pursue endeavors that take you outside of your comfort zone and are unfamiliar with you. Everyone has had some failure.

Failure isn't always a negative thing, though, as it can teach you valuable lessons and help you develop as a person.
There are few instances of people who, despite many obstacles on their path, achieved the achievement we respect and appreciate. They refused to let their fear of failing dictate how they would live.

Elon Musk, the founder and CEO of SpaceX and Tesla Motors, has failed numerous times in both his personal and professional lives. That hasn't stopped him from rising to prominence in the automotive and space transportation industries.

If you take away valuable lessons from your failures, analyze your failures to learn from them, and don't repeat the same mistakes, failure can ultimately make you a successful person.

Failure functions as a cumulative educational encounter. Every setback presents a chance for personal development and the development of a self-reflective perspective. This introspective exercise helps one steer clear of future mistakes that are similar to this one. You can pinpoint the exact choice that led to a project or circumstance going wrong and come up with plans to stop it from happening again by examining what went wrong. In order to derive meaningful lessons from failure, reflection is an essential step in the learning process.

Failure or a setback is not fatal or a cue to give up. Use your disappointments to refocus and recommit to what's important instead of slowing down or stopping. Occasionally, choosing a different course of action might result in more success and growth chances.

The road to success is unique for each person.
It doesn't imply you failed if you took a step that
helped someone else succeed even though it didn't
work out for you. It can just indicate that you will
have a different path to success. Continue to learn
and modify your behavior. You don't have to
evaluate yourself against other people.

If you make reflection a habit, you will learn
something from every experience.
Only by going back and reviewing your experiences
can you draw lessons. You will discover what
worked so you can replicate it and what didn't work
so you can adjust your approach in that way.
Developing a reflective practice will result in
epiphanies and breakthroughs.
Accept accountability for all of your achievements.
There are always going to be uncontrollable factors
that will affect your goals. That, however, does not
give you the right to whine or place the blame for
your failures on others. Accepting responsibility
entails admitting that, despite external factors, you
have the ability to alter your outcomes.

Do an assessment of your regrets before giving up.
Not everything will go as planned. Consider
whether you would regret your decision later in life

before giving up on anything. If you are certain that you won't, be certain of the rewards before giving up. Determine the necessary actions to correct your course and achieve your desired outcome if you feel that you may have to repent your choice.If you change your understanding of what constitutes a setback or failure, you may find motivation to fail your way to success.

There's a considerable possibility you will fail or face setbacks if your aims are ambitious.Your capacity to alter your viewpoint on failure will enable you to reaffirm your commitment to your goals and sustain your motivation to carry out the acts necessary to achieve your desired results.

The Value of Reflecting on Your Mistakes to Prevent Them from Happening Again

Errors can provide an invaluable chance for learning. You can learn from your mistakes and use them to sharpen your abilities and increase your knowledge.

While it's true that mistakes are unavoidable in life, they can also be a great opportunity for learning.

Everybody makes mistakes occasionally, whether it's failing to send an email or missing a deadline, but you can use a mistake to your advantage by

learning from it and improving your work by
avoiding repeating the same mistakes.

Demonstrating that you have grown from your
mistakes and that you are prepared to work towards
self-improvement will also help you gain your
employer's trust.
Furthermore, you can boost your confidence and
get over your fear of failing by taking lessons from
your failures and seeing them as valuable learning
opportunities.

Here are some strategies to help you learn from
your mistakes:
1. Own up to your errors
When you commit an error, make an effort to
acknowledge it right away and, if needed, extend
your apology. Attempting to express regret for an
error might demonstrate your regard for the
individuals the error has impacted. Additionally,
apologizing can demonstrate your regret for the
error, your willingness to accept responsibility, and
your intention to use it as a learning experience.

2. Examine your errors
Consider the mistake's origin and your solution,
making a note of your successes and failures. You
can figure out what you can do differently to make

sure the error doesn't happen again by studying and analyzing the mistake. You can use it to find solutions to any faults you make in the future.
For instance, you could figure out that you made the error of forgetting to send a crucial email if you neglected to put it on your to-do list. Then, you could list every task you have coming up in your planner.

3. Obtain feedback
Receiving comments from those in your immediate vicinity, such as your boss or coworkers, may also prove beneficial. You can become a better employee by identifying areas for improvement with the aid of constructive feedback. Mentors can also provide guidance on how to correct your errors.
For instance, you can get in touch with a mentor who used to work for you if you've made a mistake that you're not sure how to fix and ask them how they handled different circumstances. This might help you get an important perspective on your work and how to handle errors and challenging circumstances.

4. Look up lessons
Finding lessons in your failures is a crucial first step towards learning from them. For instance, you might have learned something new via a mistake.

An error could also highlight areas for skill development. You can better yourself and your job by applying the lessons you've learnt from mistakes. For instance, arriving late to a crucial meeting may indicate that you need to develop your time management abilities. If you miss a project deadline, it can be a sign that you should aim for more modest objectives.

5. Create a strategy for putting the lessons learned into practice.
As you come up with a plan to prevent repeating the same error, think about sharing it with your supervisor. In order to enhance your work and prevent repeating mistakes, you can also consider developing habits and routines. You can include particular actions in your plan, and it can be flexible. Resources and a how-to guide explaining what to do if you start making the same error can also be included.

You may set up a method to assist you in remembering all of your deadlines, for instance, if you made the mistake of overlooking a crucial one. To make sure you never forget a deadline again, an online calendar could notify you when they are about to pass.

6. Share what you've learnt with others.
In order to help others in similar roles learn from your errors, you can also think about sharing the lessons you've learnt with them. By doing this, you can help forge stronger bonds with your coworkers and prevent the same error from happening again at work. Furthermore, imparting knowledge to others can aid in retaining lessons in your memory. For instance, if you calculated a figure incorrectly on a financial statement, you may demonstrate to your coworkers how to avoid making the same error and where you made it.
Additionally, by doing this, the office can become more productive and efficient.

7. Evaluate your development
Taking stock of your progress might also assist you in seeing errors as chances for improvement. You can assess how you've incorporated teachings into your life and maintained routines. To find areas where you still need to develop, you might also consider the mistakes that you still make. Try journaling or speaking with a trusted person as a way to reflect.

8. Maintain an open mind.
Thinking of yourself as a lifelong learner is known as having a learning mentality. Having a growth mindset might assist you in seeing errors as chances for learning and development rather than as failures. Consider your mistakes to be learning opportunities that have aided in your own development rather than obsessing on past transgressions.

How to Prevent Making the Same Mistakes Again

Errors are inevitable in life and do not regard a person's identity. You will inevitably make mistakes in life, regardless of how big or tiny, strong or weak. You shouldn't fear making mistakes—in fact, what you should fear is making the same mistakes over and over again.

If you've ever made the same mistake twice, you probably understand how awful it feels. You keep hearing that voice inside your head, "I knew this would happen. Why did you let this happen again?" Sometimes, feeling bad about something you should have known better can be overwhelming. The outcome? low levels of creativity, initiative, self-worth, and confidence.

It can seriously impair your life to keep making the same mistakes over and over again. There is a method, nevertheless, to prevent you from doing them again. It's a pretty simple process; all you have to do is want to strive towards not making the same mistakes twice.

Tried-and-efficient methods that can assist you in learning from your errors and preventing future ones are listed below:

1. View errors with the proper perspective
You must first realize that mistakes are not inherently terrible in order to be able to learn from them. Making mistakes can help you identify your areas of strength and weakness.
Occasionally, the error you make holds the secret to the breakthrough you've been searching for.
Failure is merely the start of something amazing and novel—it is not the end.
As a result, try not to be too hard on yourself for your error. Recognise the potential for growth that the error gave you and capitalize on it.

2. Recognise and own your error
Acknowledging your mistakes as opportunities for growth does not equate to accepting that you

committed a mistake. You have to own up to the
fact that you made a mistake if you want to set
yourself up to never make the same one again.
You cannot rectify what you cannot accept, and you
cannot use what you do not have. When you
properly embrace it on a mental and emotional
level, you reach a significant milestone.

Many people believe and preach that mistakes are
teaching opportunities, yet you'll discover that they
are unable to draw lessons from their own mistakes
and setbacks.

Consider a past error you have made and record it.
Next, note your thoughts on why you believe it was
an error. Finally, evaluate your own behavior to
determine if you truly acknowledge that it was an
error or if you simply ignored it.
This isn't meant to bring back memories of times in
your life that you would rather forget, but rather to
help you appreciate the valuable lessons these
errors have taught you.

3. Determine the underlying cause of the error
It is one thing to own up to your mistakes and move
on. Finding the mistake's cause is the next task at
hand. On the surface, it can appear that you can
easily identify the mistake's cause.

Really, though, take a seat, consider the error, and figure out what went wrong. Continue to identify the source of each cause you identify until you have identified the primary reason for the error.
For instance, you might easily blame inadequate preparation if you didn't pass the examination.

However, that is not the real reason; instead, you need to ask yourself what exactly led to the inadequate planning.
Was it because you did something else or watched films for a while? After that, you discover what led you to watch films when you ought to have been studying. Did a friend put you under pressure? Was it your own lack of motivation?
Until you identify the actual reason of the error, keep asking yourself these questions.

4. Deal with the root issue
You have undoubtedly fixed a lot of errors just to discover that they keep happening.
That is because you didn't address the mistake's underlying fundamental cause, only the mistake's surface-level issue. Make sure to address the real cause of the error and draw lessons from it. Create and exert the necessary effort to guarantee that the mistake's underlying cause is dealt with.

That way, you can practically guarantee that such an error won't happen again.
It is crucial that you understand that you can't be sure the error won't happen again unless you've addressed it appropriately.

Most of the time, you know exactly what has to be done, but you lack the willpower and tenacity to achieve it. You should know that in order to make the best decisions for your own life, you must be able to inspire yourself. You are capable of taking care of yourself more than anyone else is.
Thus, get ready, step up to the plate, and make a commitment to improving yourself.

5. Put your lesson in writing.
Every error and every setback offers a chance to gain knowledge. Every time you make a mistake, make sure to address the underlying cause of the error to stop it from happening again by following these steps. Then, record the lesson you learned from the mistake.

You have to learn to document your experiences so that you can impart them to others if you want to achieve great things and reach higher altitudes. Maintain the proper perspective on your mistakes, deal with the underlying causes of each one you

make, and make sure you document all of the
lessons you take away from them. You will be on the
way to bigger things if you do this.

Make a list of the things you have learned from your
mistakes. And list the finest tactics and solutions
you would use to reach your desired level of
success.
Seek to learn in life rather than to win; you will
most likely find that you win much more in the
process of learning.
Never give up on a dream because you don't believe
you have the necessary skills or background.

Each of us has had to grow from our failures and
keep trying until we achieve.
It is our life's narrative.

Thus, don't be scared of failing. Adapt to new
information.
All of the experiences are a part of the learning
curve of life.
It is unavoidable to fail at times; it is a natural
aspect of being human.
We are erratic people who frequently depend more
on their gut feeling than on hard data or give in to
overconfidence. But, your chances of long-term
success will undoubtedly rise if you can change the

way you view failure and see every "fail" as a teaching moment. We are only human, after all, and reality does not always match perception.
What you might consider a failure could be viewed by others as a small setback.
Rise above your setbacks, take lessons from your errors, and take comfort in the knowing that you will soon have the chance to make the correct decisions.

Chapter Three: Perseverance and Resilience (picking oneself up after failing)

The ability to successfully adjust to harsh or hard life situations is referred to as resilience. The capacity to persevere through hardship, recover, and develop in spite of challenging circumstances in life is resilience. Being resilient does not absolve one from hardship, suffering, or mental turmoil. Being resilient means having the capacity to overcome emotional hardship.

It's crucial to remember that developing your skill set to become resilient takes time. You must put in the effort to develop resilience, and you'll probably encounter obstacles along the way. It depends on both internal factors (like social support) and external factors (like communication skills and self-esteem).

The ability to process and overcome adversity makes resilience crucial. Resilient people don't handle stress well and may resort to bad coping techniques. To overcome obstacles and solve issues, resilient people lean on their assets and networks of support.

Resilience can be classified into several categories or sorts, though it is commonly used to refer to general adaptability and coping skills:

Resilience in Psychology
The capacity to adjust or mentally handle uncertainties, difficulties, and misfortune is known as psychological resilience, according to researchers. Sometimes people refer to it as "mental fortitude."
People with psychological resilience learn coping mechanisms and techniques that help them get through a crisis with composure and focus and move on without suffering from distressing or anxiety-inducing long-term effects.

Resilience in Emotions The ability to maintain realistic optimism in the face of adversity is known as emotional resilience.
According to the Children's Society, each person has a different emotional coping mechanism for stress and misfortune. Certain individuals are inherently more or less sensitive to shifts. Some

people experience a wave of emotions in response to an event, whereas others do not.

People with emotional resilience know why they feel the way they do.

In times of crisis, they maintain a healthy dose of realistic optimism and make proactive use of both internal and external resources to see things through. They possess the ability to effectively and positively regulate both their internal and external stressors.

Physical Resilience

Physical resilience pertains to the body's capacity to adjust to various situations, sustain energy and power, and recuperate swiftly and effectively. It's the capacity of an individual to carry out daily tasks and heal from injuries, illnesses, or other physical demands.

Studies reveal that when people age and face health problems and physical stressors, physical resilience is crucial to their overall well-being.

Physical resilience is influenced by a number of factors, including a healthy lifestyle, relationships with friends and neighbors, deep breathing, adequate rest and recovery time, and participation in fun activities.

Collective Adaptability

The term "community resilience" describes a group's capacity to react to and bounce back from unfavorable circumstances, including natural catastrophes, violent crimes, difficult economic times, and other obstacles that affect the group as a whole.

Adversity comes in many forms for people in life. Personal crises might include things like disease, the death of a loved one, abuse, bullying, losing one's work, and unstable finances. We all live in a world where terrible things like war, natural catastrophes, mass shootings, terrorist attacks, and pandemics happen frequently. Individuals must learn coping mechanisms and coping strategies for really difficult life situations.

The concepts of resilience theory deal with how people respond to and adjust to difficult situations such as risk, loss, change, and adversity. Numerous disciplines, including psychiatry, human development, and change management, have investigated resilience theory.

According to resilience theory, you can develop your potential to practice resilience; it's not a fixed trait. Furthermore, it's not always the same; you might show a lot of resilience in the face of one problem but find it more difficult to remain resilient in the face of another stressor.

By altering specific attitudes and behaviors, people can tap into their resilience with the aid of flexibility, adaptability, and tenacity. According to research, students who feel that social and intellectual skills may be developed and enhanced are more resilient, doing better and exhibiting a reduced stress reaction in the face of adversity.

According to experts, resilience entails the following ideas:

Thankfulness

Kindness

Acceptance

Meaning

Forgiveness

Techniques for Creating and Strengthening Resilience in the Face of Failure

Building resilience is a complicated and individual process. Being more resilient requires a blend of external resources and inner capabilities; there is no one-size-fits-all method.

APA lists the following as some of the major elements that go into a person's personal resilience:

The perspectives and interactions a person has with the world

The social resources' quality and availability

Particular coping mechanisms

Building resilience is a result of several things, and overcoming adversity is not something that can be accomplished by following a set of instructions. Additionally, resilience is a quality that develops with time.
Positive self-perceptions, strong interpersonal ties, and family cohesiveness were protective factors against depression in teenagers at risk in a prior longitudinal study.

Resilience theory states that the following additional elements contribute to resilience development:

Social assistance
According to research, a person's social networks—which might include their friends, neighbors, personal or extended relatives, and organizations—help them become resilient when faced with adversity or catastrophe.

Self-worth

In the face of difficulty, a strong sense of self-worth and self-assurance in one's abilities helps prevent emotions of powerlessness.

Possessing coping and problem-solving abilities is beneficial when one must face hardship and persevere through adversity. Studies indicate that the application of constructive coping strategies (e.g., sharing and optimism) can enhance resilience more than the use of destructive strategies.

Talents in communication

People who can communicate effectively and clearly are better equipped to mobilize resources, ask for aid, and take action. Studies indicate that those who are able to engage with others, empathetically, and who instill confidence and trust in others are generally more resilient.

Control of emotions

Research on resilience theory suggests that people can use resilience at other times as well, not just in the face of extreme hardship. As people deal with a variety of stressors on a daily basis, it intensifies. People who possess resilience are able to handle pain, misfortune, and adversity with emotional fortitude.

People that are resilient make use of their assets, abilities, and qualities to get beyond obstacles and bounce back from failures.

Individuals who are not resilient are more likely to resort to unhealthy coping mechanisms (such self-medication, avoidance, and isolation) when they feel overwhelmed or powerless.

According to a study, those who possess these traits—resilience, coping skills, and emotional intelligence—are more likely to be happy in life and to be in better health than those who do not.

People with resilience are able to accept their circumstances, change with them, and go on.

It's crucial to remember that developing your skill set to become resilient takes time. You must put in the effort to develop resilience, and you'll probably encounter obstacles along the way.

It depends on both internal factors (such as social support and the resources you have access to) and external factors (such as personal behaviors and abilities, such as communication and self-esteem).

Being resilient does not absolve one from hardship, suffering, or mental turmoil. Overcoming emotional sorrow and pain is a sign of resilience.

Here are five strategies for building resilience:
1. Relationships: Studies show that those who have a robust support network find it easier to deal with difficulties. Leaders who take the time to establish and preserve wholesome marriages and families consequently perform better at work. They are difficult to divert from their path. They can get back "on track" more quickly if they are.
Developing connections with those who are optimistic, driven, supportive, and show you care also helps to fortify your network of support. Stay away from those who deplete you. Spend less time with those who mainly whine, place the blame on others, or lack drive. They are not adept at overcoming hardship.

2. Increase Self-Efficacy: Develop a "can do" attitude. The most effective leaders act, have a purpose for acting, and have faith that their actions will yield outcomes.
The main way to develop this feeling of "can do" is to concentrate on what you can truly accomplish in a certain circumstance. This contrasts with concentrating on outside factors that are beyond your control.
A lot of people have a tendency to see themselves as victims or powerless in life. People are continually hindered from acting by something or someone.

"The man" or "the system" is impeding or holding them back.

While some people may give opposition, "can do" leaders are aware of this and concentrate on what they can accomplish to achieve their desired outcomes. They consequently continue to increase their knowledge, skills, and power.

3. Positivity: As Zig Ziglar once said, develop into a "good finder." Developing an intentional practice of thankfulness is among the most transformative and potent actions you will ever undertake. Learning to appreciate others and express that appreciation to them is closely tied to this. It's one of the most straightforward yet effective leadership mindsets. A crucial component of resilience is the capacity to search for and recognise the positive aspects of adversity or setback.

4. Vision: Keep in mind your goals and "Why." It is foolish to suffer for the sake of suffering. It is essential to have a clear idea of what you are attempting to build or safeguard.
Keeping your "Why" for persevering through a struggle front and center will keep you motivated and focused. In moments when you might feel

helpless or powerless, it gives your life purpose and direction.

5. Progress Attitude: When difficulties are seen as chances to learn and develop, they stop being "all negative" experiences and start being occasions for progress. Moving from attempting to escape or survive obstacles to consciously seeking the teachings they present on a personal level.
They enter into the environment after realizing its truths, believing that doing so will make them stronger and help them flourish.

Additionally, see obstacles as chances to try out novel viewpoints or strategies. Challenges send us into reactive mode far too frequently. Growth is possible when one takes the initiative to investigate alternative approaches to, or perceptions of, this scenario.

One chooses to be resilient: They search for reasons for gratitude and appreciation. They reaffirm their sense of direction to themselves. They're looking to grow.
Choose resiliency. It will bring you joy. You and your group will recover more quickly as a result.

Perseverance's Power and Significance

Let's explore the transformational potential of tenacity and learn how it may help us achieve greatness.

Initially Getting Past Adversity: The ability to persevere gives us the fortitude required to meet challenges head-on. We will inevitably face obstacles in life, but those who don't give up will not be overcome by failure. Rather, they see setbacks as chances for improvement and persevere through them with steadfast resolve. We may gain the resilience to persevere through adversity, learn from our mistakes, and come out stronger and wiser by developing a persisting mindset.

Goal-setting and Goal-Achievement: Perseverance is the engine that drives us to reach our objectives. It gives us the confidence to set high goals and work tirelessly to achieve them. We get a little bit closer to our goals with perseverance, hard effort, and a steadfast commitment to success. Perseverance ensures that we continue on course in the face of difficulties and setbacks by keeping us resilient, driven, and focused. We gain momentum and go closer to realizing our goals with every little step ahead.

Personal Development: Perseverance is a key component in the process of personal development. By persevering through challenging circumstances, we push our limits and uncover our hidden talents and qualities. It helps us believe in ourselves since we know we are capable of overcoming obstacles and achieving our goals. Additionally, perseverance fosters self-control, tolerance, and flexibility, which help us acquire important life skills that benefit us in many facets of our lives.

Building Resilience: Resilience, or the capacity to overcome adversity, is a sign of persistence. Persistent people see setbacks and disappointments as opportunities for growth rather than obstacles to trip over. They take what they've learned, tweak as necessary, and move forward with fresh vigor. By developing resilience via persistence, we may more easily navigate through life's uncertainties and make sure that setbacks don't stop us from pursuing our ultimate goal.

Motivating Others to Strive for Excellence: Strive for excellence has a significant effect on others around us as well as on ourselves. We encourage and inspire people to pursue their own aspirations and goals by demonstrating the strength of tenacity. Our steadfast commitment and fortitude serve as a source of inspiration for people who might be going through difficult times of their own.

We have the power to empower and encourage others by our deeds, and when we do so, good things can happen in our communities and beyond.

Ultimately, persistence is a force that pushes us ahead, enabling us to break through obstacles and realize our limitless potential. Its advantages permeate every area of our lives and go well beyond individual accomplishments.

We may overcome adversity, accomplish our goals, and begin out on a road of resilience and personal growth by developing a persisting attitude. Thus, let's embrace tenacity as a necessary tool for success and encourage others to follow suit. We can create a world where dreams come true and tenacity flourishes if we work together.

Resilience involves more than just getting back up after a setback; it also involves growing stronger, learning from each experience, and adapting. It's the steadfast conviction that failure is merely a bump in the road leading to triumph rather than the end. It's the courage to get back up, pick ourselves up, and move forth with a fresh lease on life.

When everything around us seems to be working against us, perseverance is the will and dedication to our vision. It's the will to keep going after our objectives in the face of overwhelming obstacles and not give up. It's the will to persevere, driven by the conviction that achievement is imminent.

This crucial quality, which shows a person's perseverance, resilience, and commitment to reaching their goals, is frequently the key to success.
The will to accomplish a goal is referred to as determination.
The quality of tenacity is the capacity to continue despite difficulties and disappointments.
Conversely, resilience is the ability to overcome misfortune and turn things around.
Perseverance motivates people to keep going forward and keep their eyes on the prize in the face of difficulty.

The Value Of Perseverance In Achieving Success

Unwavering perseverance is crucial on the road to success.It is impossible to exaggerate how crucial persistence is to success. It frequently serves as the impetus for both professional and personal development since it gives people the will to overcome obstacles and push past boundaries. Because they consistently push themselves to attain new heights despite hurdles, those with strong perseverance are more likely to succeed in their endeavors.

The key to enduring life's journey is endurance rather than speed. Similar to a marathon, where endurance is prioritized over pace, is perseverance. There will inevitably be ups and downs on the trip through life, but people may overcome these obstacles and reach their objectives by working hard and being flexible.

Individuals can embrace the power of perseverance and utilize it to propel their journey towards personal and professional accomplishment by realizing that the path to success is not a sprint but rather a test of resolve and commitment.

Sustainability in Self-Development
It promotes self-assurance and pushes you past
self-doubt.
Self-doubt is one of the largest obstacles to any kind
of success. Perseverance cultivates assurance to face
obstacles and helps get over self-doubt. Your
self-confidence is boosted when you overcome
obstacles and see the fruits of your labor.

Creating Assurance
Every accomplishment and challenge faced along
the way helps to build self-confidence in the
perseverance path. You come to understand that
persistence is the key to overcoming even the most
difficult obstacles.

It Fosters Individual Development
No matter how difficult anything gets, perseverance
teaches you a lot about yourself. You discover your
actual potential. Perseverance can help one grow
personally in this way, for example.
It turns challenges into chances for personal growth
and self-discovery.
While personal growth is a continuous process, it
quickens when faced with challenges.
You pick up new abilities.
You pick up fresh experiences.
You learn new things about who you are.

Together, these components improve your personal growth.
Accept obstacles.
These are your opportunities to develop.

It Promotes Personality Growth
Maintaining focus on difficult activities encourages the formation of fundamental principles. These principles include a strong work ethic, devotion, and dedication.

As you keep going, you realize how important it is to: Have a strong commitment to your objectives, working diligently every day and demonstrating commitment even in difficult times.
These principles are essential for both professional and personal development.

It Quickens the Development of Skills
The adage "Practice makes perfect" is well-known. Persistence is essential in this situation. It motivates you to practice regularly, which will improve your talents.
You can practice a skill till you master it if you have perseverance in it. Your abilities will improve and become more refined the more you practice.

When you don't get it right, don't give up; keep trying.

Persistence in a Growth Mindset
Persistence is a vital ally in the development of a growth mentality. It strengthens the conviction that your skills and intelligence are malleable and can be developed.
You realize that you are not limited by your existing ability when you persevere.
Rather, it helps you realize that you can push the boundaries of your abilities and improve them with regular work, smart tactics, and insightful feedback from others.
It works similarly to how sunlight and water enable a seed to grow into a tree, transforming potential into strength.

Promoting Growth
The allure of a growth mindset is its capacity to alter the way you view mistakes and obstacles. You start to perceive them as stepping stones on the path to growth rather than as obstacles or destination points.
They turn into opportunities for learning that aid in pinpointing your areas in need of development. Falling down is not the important thing; what

matters is getting back up, picking yourself up, and taking what you learned from it.

Thus, even in the midst of difficulties, a development mentality fostered by persistence sees a diversion rather than a dead end and leads to success.

Always try to get better. Making even a tiny improvement is a step in the right direction.

It Fosters an Attitude of Constant Improvement
We learn to believe that there is always room for improvement via perseverance. You see every obstacle you face as a chance to grow and learn. When you have an attitude of constant progress, you don't accept mediocrity. Rather, you make an effort to improve every day.

Perseverance in One's Own Talents
It Increases Resilience
Obstacles are unavoidable. The most important thing is your capacity for recovery, which is based on tenacity.

Resilience is more than just getting beyond setbacks; it also involves pushing through them with more vigor. You become powerful and capable of overcoming obstacles because of your tenacity.Don't give up when you encounter a setback. Go back and get stronger.

It Improves Your Ability to Solve Problems
Creative Thinking: Overcoming hurdles is a common experience for those who persevere. As you look for answers to the current difficulties, this promotes creative thinking.
Emphasis on Solutions Adopting a solution-focused mindset is facilitated by perseverance. You become more adept at concentrating on fixes than on issues. This improves your ability to solve problems, which is advantageous in a number of ways.

It Enhances Capabilities of Effective Communication
You can communicate your ideas and views more clearly if you have perseverance. You develop clear communication skills as you work towards your objectives and express your needs, wants, and ideas.
Perseverance may improve your communication abilities whether you're expressing your feelings, negotiating a transaction, or defending your position.
Engage in active hearing. It's essential to clear communication.

Perseverance and Persistence in Work Ethics

It Incorporates a Hardworking Work Ethics
One of the most important characteristics of successful people is their conscientious work ethic, which is developed through perseverance. When you continue, you live the value of hard effort rather than just seeing it.

You get to understand the value of being dependable and making an effort every day, no matter how little. This insight is not something that appears out of nowhere; persistence shapes and refines it.

In the end, persistence is what teaches you the real worth of grit, sweat, and the daily grind.

Developing a conscientious work ethic via persistence has profound effects on your life.

It functions as a key that unlocks doors to success in a variety of areas, including:

Your profession

Your learning

Your individual goals

A strong work ethic is similar to a rudder that guides your life's ship towards success. It serves as the catalyst to keep you advancing towards your goals.

An industrious work ethic cultivated through persistence can therefore pave the way, whether you're working on a challenging project, preparing for a significant test, or pursuing a personal goal.Continue working on the assignment even if it seems difficult. Your diligence will be rewarded.

It Increases Attention
Perseverance has a profound impact on your capacity to focus your attention and efforts on your objectives. It focuses your energies on the things that are really important, much like a laser beam. Perseverance serves as a reminder to keep on track when faced with distractions. It's the inner voice reminding you to focus on the goal. Perseverance becomes the anchor that keeps you stable in the middle of all the distractions when you sharpen your concentration.

Today's fast-paced society might make it difficult to maintain concentration. But if you stick with it, you can master the skill of narrowing your concentration.
Even though the path to reaching your objectives may be convoluted, your steadfast determination, strengthened by persistence, serves as a headlight. Perseverance maintains your attention firm and clear, illuminating the path ahead even when it

becomes hazy. It is the compass that keeps you focused and constantly points in the direction of your objectives.Engage in mindfulness. It might facilitate sharper attention.

It Facilitates the Development of Good Habits
Perseverance is essential for developing healthy behaviors that promote wellbeing and personal development. You are more likely to develop habits that reflect your level of dedication to a goal.
These routines could include learning consistently, exercising frequently, or maintaining a balanced diet. But one thing is certain—they support your objectives and get stronger the more you stick with them.
Perseverance shapes your habits, which in turn determines your life.

Developing Durable Habits
Forming new habits requires patience, time, and constant effort—just like sculpting a sculpture. In this process, perseverance is the sculptor's tool; it chisels away at the behavior gradually until it becomes a routine part of who you are.

It Helps Get Rid of Procrastination
Motivating Action: Consider tenacity as the antithesis of procrastination. The hero is the one who motivates you to take action and go forward, even when all you want to do is curl up with a nice book or binge-watch your favorite show.
When procrastination shouts, "Do it tomorrow," perseverance whispers, "You can do it." When you're drowning in the rain of inaction, it's the spark that ignites the fire of action.
Fighting Passivity Like quicksand, procrastination can drag you down and prevent you from achieving your objectives. It stands in the way of your achievement.
Now, though, what? Having perseverance is what keeps you afloat. It gives you the motivation to act, get beyond obstacles, and keep going. It's the ability that makes you say "I'll do it now" instead of "I'll do it later."
Begin modestly. Big improvement can come from little steps.

Perseverance in Reaching Objectives
It Makes Goal Achievement Possible
You have to work consistently to reach your goals. A lone try is insufficient. Perseverance is the ability to move forward in the face of adversity and delayed progress towards one's objectives.

Overcoming Obstacles: If you don't have persistence, you might give up at the first obstacle. But if you keep going, you can overcome these obstacles.

You attempt novel tactics.

You seek assistance.

You exert more force.

Perseverance ultimately enables you to accomplish your objectives.

Recall your initial motivation. It will sustain your enthusiasm.

It Sustains a Passion

Our desire to pursue our goals and interests is fuelled by passion. But it can be difficult to keep this passion alive when things are tough. Through perseverance, we may make sure that our passion doesn't fade in the face of difficulty.

You maintain the spark of passion by persevering. You maintain your motivation because you are passionate about your objectives even in the face of difficulty.

Individuals that possess passion are frequently more dedicated, ebullient, and content in both their personal and professional spheres.

It Improves Quality of Life
Being persistent is compatible with living a happy
life. It encourages you to pursue your objectives,
uphold your moral principles, and build a life you
can be proud of.
You feel more content and happy when you work
towards your objectives and see the results of your
efforts.

It Promotes the Development of Significant
Legacies
Establishing Standards With perseverance, you can
leave a lasting legacy. It assists you in establishing
an example of perseverance, hard effort, and
dedication that others can follow.
Leaving a Legacy: Your tenacity can inspire people
to follow their aspirations and have an enduring
impact on others.

Persistence in Wellness and Health
Advantages of Mental Health
Mental health can be greatly impacted by
perseverance. People who have a strong sense of
perseverance and resolve are better able to handle
obstacles and failures. This may result in enhanced:
Stress Reduction Suffering through challenging
circumstances can make people better at managing
stress, which lowers the risk of stress-related

mental health conditions including depression and anxiety.

Self-Regard: Overcoming challenges and reaching personal objectives can boost confidence and self-worth, which in turn has a beneficial effect on mental health.

Control of Emotions As people learn to navigate through difficult emotional situations and maintain a healthy balance in their emotions, perseverance can help people build greater emotional regulation skills.

Advantages for Physical Health
Perseverance can have favorable effects on physical health in addition to mental health benefits. Important advantages for physical wellness include:

Enhanced Fitness Compliance Exercise regimen maintenance calls for commitment and self-control. People who possess perseverance are more likely to maintain their exercise routine, which improves their general health and physical fitness.

Injury Avoidance: Through perseverance, people can lower their risk of injury by continuing to practice appropriate form, technique, and precautions when engaging in physical activity.

Fostering Healthful Behaviors: Healthy behaviors like stress management, enough sleep, and good eating frequently call for consistent work and dedication. Maintaining these constructive behaviors can be facilitated by the development of perseverance.

Persistence in Interpersonal and Communal Relationships

It Encourages Beatitude Perseverance and cultivates patience, which is necessary for long-term success.

Perseverance teaches you that things take time to happen. It teaches you to wait with perseverance. Because it teaches us that great and meaningful outcomes require time and consistent work, perseverance fosters patience.

It Aids in the Resolution of Conflicts

In times of conflict, perseverance pushes us to work towards a resolution rather than running from or intensifying them. Perseverance is the key to transforming conflict into harmony.

Perseverance in the face of conflict encourages a positive strategy. It promotes communication, comprehension, and flexibility.

Example: Disagreements will inevitably arise in relationships. Nonetheless, if you are persistent, you may resolve conflicts and build your connection in the process.

It Fortifies Moral Principles
Characteristics like bravery, tenacity, and humility are developed with perseverance. conquering obstacles and conquering them fortifies your moral principles and character.
You can develop into a more responsible, understanding, and patient person by persevering. You are aware of the importance of integrity, honesty, and respect.
Retain your integrity at all times. It is the foundation of a solid moral personality.

The Value of Equilibrium While Holding Fast, Take Care of Yourself

Success requires striking a balance between tenacity and one's own well-being, which includes both physical and emotional health.
In addition to ensuring mental health through stress management, nourishing relationships, and self-compassion, regular exercise, adequate sleep, and a healthy diet energize us for goal pursuit.

Physical and mental health are related; problems with one can affect the other. It is essential to put one's general well-being first while pursuing objectives.
Acknowledge When to Change Direction and Help Others
Sometimes it's a good idea to give up on an unreachable or dangerous project or goal; this isn't a sign of failure but rather an opportunity to grow and go in different ways.
Suffering under such circumstances can: Damage relationships; induce stress
effect on health

Knowing when to change course or give up is essential. Encouraging others to achieve their goals should be combined with consideration for their welfare and being prepared to suggest a different course of action if needed. Better conflict resolution, personal development, and healthier relationships are all facilitated by this. Perseverance is ultimately your best tool for success. It functions similarly to a muscle that becomes stronger the more obstacles you face. It fortifies your resolve, boosts your self-esteem, and molds your personality. It's important to remember that getting through difficult times is only one aspect of growing, learning, and becoming better.

Thus, don't be afraid to take on new tasks or let setbacks deter you. Always remember that perseverance is about creating the life you really desire, not merely about achieving your objectives. Keep going, and don't forget to enjoy the journey!

Chapter Four: Getting Rid of the Fear of Failure

Many of us at some point in our lives set out on a path to overcome the fear of failing. It's a road paved with wisdom, self-awareness, and enormous growth possibilities. Although this fear can prevent us from realizing our full potential, we can learn to accept failure as a necessary step on the path to success by adopting the appropriate mentality and technique.

Sometimes the fear of failing might be so great that it overpowers the desire to achieve. Many people unintentionally undermine their chances of success because they are insecure about making mistakes.

This is undoubtedly something that many of us have encountered at some point. Fear of failing may be crippling; it can prevent us from doing, and we're likely to miss some great opportunities along the way.

Have you ever chosen not to try something at all because you were so terrified you wouldn't succeed? Or has your fear of failing caused you to unconsciously undercut your own attempts to prevent the chance of a more serious failure?

This is undoubtedly something that many of us have encountered at some point. The dread of failing can be crippling; it can prevent us from acting and prevent us from taking action. But if we let fear to keep us from moving forward in life, we're probably going to pass up some fantastic chances.

It is nearly impossible to go through life without failing at some point. Those who live this way most often lead very cautious lives that lead nowhere. In other words, they're not actually breathing.

The great thing about failure, though, is that we get to choose how we choose to view it. We have the option to view failure as "the end of the world" or as evidence of our own inadequacies. Alternatively, we might view failure as the fantastic teaching tool that it frequently is. Whenever we make a mistake, we have the option to search for the lesson that should be learned. These lessons are crucial because they help us develop and prevent us from repeating the same mistakes. We are only stopped by our own failures.

Finding successful people with a history of failure is not difficult. For instance:

Most people agree that Michael Jordan is among the all-time best basketball players. Despite this, his coach dismissed him from the high school basketball team because he was seen to lack sufficient skill.

Harvard University turned down one of the wealthiest and most prosperous business people in the world, Warren Buffet.

The founder of the Virgin empire, Richard Branson, dropped out of high school. In life, most of us will trip and fall.

We may make poor choices, and doors will be slammed in our faces. But what if, after being cut from that squad, Michael Jordan had given up on his dream of being a professional basketball player? What if Richard Branson had paid attention to those who advised him that he could never accomplish anything significant without a high school diploma.

Consider the chances you will lose if you allow your mistakes to deter you. We can learn things about ourselves via failure that we never would have otherwise. For example, failing might reveal your strength as a person. You may meet your best friends via failure, or you may find unanticipated inspiration to achieve. Good ideas frequently emerge only after a setback.

To achieve in life, one must embrace those realizations and take lessons from them.

We will avoid potentially dangerous circumstances out of fear of failing, but failure-related fear will also prevent us from realizing our greatest potential. Fear of failing prevents us from attempting, breeds self-doubt, stops us from moving forward, and sometimes even causes us to act immorally.

The following are the primary causes of failure-related fear:

1. Early Life Environment: Fear of failure can be a learnt behavior if it was instilled in you as a child and you were taught that it is wrong. Emotional and

psychological problems including panic attacks, low self-esteem, anxiety, despair, and shame can result from this fear of failing.It's possible that you have encountered someone who imposed rules based on fear and gave you ultimatums.

2. Perfectionism: People who are perfectionists don't attempt because they think failing is so awful and embarrassing. When you move beyond your comfort zone, it might be daunting. Similar to this, perfectionism may also have its roots in early life if the notion of anything less than ideal was seen as a sign of failure. Usually, the ego drives us to strive for excellence and our wanting to please others.

3. Over-Personalization: Our egos might cause us to identify ourselves too much with our mistakes. You can worry about being perceived as a failure because you think that your mistakes have a big influence on how other people see you.

We must first define "failure" in order to identify the root causes of fear of failing.Because we all have distinct standards, morals, and worldviews, we all define failure differently. For someone else, a failure could just be an excellent teaching moment.Get over your fear of failing and keep going to accomplish your objectives.

At some point or another, a lot of us fear failing. However, fear of failing (also known as "atychiphobia") manifests itself when we allow it to prevent us from taking the actions necessary to go forward and accomplish our objectives.

Numerous factors might contribute to fear of failure. For example, some people's causes include having parents who are strict or unsupportive. They carry into adulthood the bad emotions they had as children, when they were frequently belittled or embarrassed.

Another factor could be going through a stressful experience in your life. Say, for instance, that you performed appallingly in a significant presentation you had to give in front of a sizable audience a number of years ago. It could have been such a bad encounter that you developed a fear of failing in other things.

If you have a fear of failing, you can experience some or all of the following symptoms:

A reluctance to try new or challenging things. Self-sabotage can manifest in a variety of ways, including overly anxious behavior, procrastination, and failing to achieve goals.

The frequent use of negative statements such as "I'm not smart enough to get on that team" or "I'll never be good enough to get that promotion" is indicative of low self-esteem or lack of confidence.The tendency to only take on projects that you are positive you can finish successfully and flawlessly is known as perfectionism.

It's important to recognise that we could fail in anything we try. Embracing that opportunity requires courage, but it also results in constantly resisting your fear of failing.

Examine the worst-case situation. In certain circumstances, the worst-case scenario can be truly catastrophic, in which case it would make sense to be afraid of failing. In other instances, though, this worst-case scenario might not be all that horrible, and releasing this can be beneficial.

Have a backup plan - If you're nervous about doing anything new, having a "Plan B" ready will give you greater confidence to proceed.

How to Quit Living in Fear: Techniques for Dealing with the Fear of Failing

You may find it difficult to set objectives if you are terrified of failing. However, goals aid in defining our life's purpose. Without objectives, our destination is uncertain.

A lot of professionals advise using visualization as a strong technique while creating goals. Thinking about your life after you've accomplished your objective will help you stay motivated. Those who dread failure, however, may experience the opposite effects from visualization.

According to research, asking people to visualize their objectives and accomplishments frequently leaves them in a very gloomy attitude. These people are those who fear failure.What else can you do in its place?To begin, make a few modest objectives. These ought to be moderately difficult but not too objective. Consider these objectives as "early wins" that will make you feel more confident.

Your sense of identity and self-worth may be significantly impacted by your success-related emotions. Therefore, when success seems elusive, the fear of failing might impede professional advancement.

Overcoming your fear of failing, however, is a crucial step towards both your career and personal development. It has been demonstrated that facing your fear of failing will help you overcome it.

Let's look at these simple actions you may do to get started on the path to developing self-confidence and overcoming your fear of failing.

1. Determine the Source of the Fear: Which of the potential causes of your fear of failing strike a chord with you? Put your thoughts on paper and make an effort to comprehend the anxiety from the perspective of an outsider.

Maybe a deep-seated insecurity or something that happened to you as a youngster is the source of your fear. The terror loses some of its strength when the source is identified.

2. Reframe Your Beliefs About Your Objective: Sometimes, an all-or-nothing mindset leaves you with nothing. Have a specific goal in mind, but don't forget to incorporate learning something.

Having a growth mentality, which focuses on learning and improvement, greatly reduces the likelihood of failure. Failure is a part of that philosophy, but as long as they fulfil their goal of presenting amazing stories, all of the setbacks are simply chances to improve.

3. Develop a Positive Outlook: Although success is highly valued in our society, it's crucial to acknowledge that even the most accomplished individuals experience setbacks. A newspaper reportedly sacked Walt Disney on the grounds that

they didn't think he was creative. He later founded an unsuccessful animation studio. Disney is a household name now because he never gave up.

Disney would not have made it if he had taken the negative reviews seriously. You must become aware of your negative self-talk and pinpoint your triggers. The voice in your head greatly influences your actions. Positive information about the circumstance and yourself should take the place of negative ideas. You'll be able to write a fresh mental screenplay that you can refer to whenever you sense pessimism beginning to surface.

4. See Every Possible Result: You may decide against choosing a new job out of fear of the unknown. Consider the advantages and disadvantages and the possible outcomes while making such a significant life decision. Gaining insight into potential outcomes could aid in your recovery.

5. Examine the Worst-Case Scenario: Occasionally, the worst-case scenario might be utterly disastrous. Often times, a negative event won't spell the end of the world. Determining how horrible the worst-case situation would be in the overall scheme of things is crucial. We occasionally give circumstances more weight than they merit. Generally speaking, a failure can be recovered from.

6. Keep a Backup Plan: Having a backup plan never hurts. After the worst has occurred, rushing to find a solution is the last thing you want to do. It's wise to follow the old proverb, "Hope for the best, prepare for the worst."

You feel more confident to move forward and take measured risks when you have a backup plan.

7. Take A Lesson From Anything That Happens: Even an unfavorable circumstance might present a wonderful chance to improve and advance.

If you look closely enough, you'll eventually see the bright side. You can overcome your fear of failure once you realize that "failure" is a chance for personal development rather than a fatal blow.

We may begin overcoming our fear of failure by understanding its origins and changing the way we think about it. It's simpler to get over anxiety when you see failure as an opportunity for personal development and you've considered all the scenarios.

Remain upbeat, prepare a fallback strategy, and take lessons from every mishap. Rather than bringing you shame, your mistakes will serve as a source of knowledge and motivation.

Sometimes setbacks might be a disguised benefit. Take decisive action towards your aspirations and long-term objectives.

So how do we handle the dread of not succeeding? Listed below are sure methods to help you transform your anxiety into drive for good:

Improve your emotional intelligence first: Understanding your emotions, being able to express them, and being able to limit their impact are all components of emotional intelligence. Indeed, it IS able to be learned!

Keep a journal of your elevated feelings during the workday to help you become more conscious of yourself. Put them in writing and think of them as information about your triggers and your reaction to fear. Next, make the most of them by developing the ability to predict their responses and lessen the impact they have on your goal-setting and decision-making. It requires a great deal of compassion, time, and tolerance. But the work is worthwhile!

2. Have faith in your instincts: Your instincts are crucial when it comes to fear. You must learn to have faith in your own judgment and in yourself. Consider it a sign to look more closely at a decision if it makes you feel afraid. Take the initiative to solve problems and ask yourself the more difficult questions. Is there a valid fear? What could possibly go wrong? What does that say for YOU, if this thing comes to pass? See fear as a cue to learn more and identify the real cause of your uneasiness. You can figure out where to go from there once you know the root.

3. Educate yourself: Knowledge is a powerful tool for managing fear. Learning and gathering information is one of the most important strategies to get over anxiety. Gaining knowledge can help you feel more in control and offer you a breather, whether it's by reading about a recent development in your field or learning a new skill that seems a little outside of your comfort zone.

4. Request backup: This is today's most crucial piece of advice. Seeking assistance is crucial in combating the fear of failing. Having a mentor is essential for business ownership, so while you develop and produce, it should be your top goal to have someone on your side.

The most significant effects come from support because it fosters learning, problem-solving, and self-awareness. Asking for assistance is the best use of your resources. Moreover, requesting reinforcements can present a fantastic chance to mentor additional people. It teaches you how to operate your business with humility and delegation.

Seek out this type of community through mentorship programmes, industry associations, local business networks, or even just team dynamics!

You should know that you're not alone if you're now experiencing anxiety over your business failing.

Every nearby business owner is going through the same thing as you are; we've been there. We all deal with fear in different ways, so you have to figure out what works for you. Just remember that sometimes, what we seem to be failing, is really an opportunity. Find that chance and change your perception of failure!

It's normal to be afraid of failing, but you can push past short-term obstacles and keep working towards your objectives. The actions listed above can help you get over your fear of failing so that you can pursue a successful profession.

1. Admit it: The idea of "facing your fear" is not particularly new. But dealing with a fear of heights or spiders is far easier than dealing with a fear of failing.

2. Make it external: There are moments when facing fear is an uphill battle. The voice of uncertainty and negativity will never go away, no matter how hard we attempt to face it or will our way out of it. This second tactic focuses more on learning to live with fear than it does on eliminating it.

3. Disregard it: The first two methods for conquering fear, Face It and Externalize It, dealt with how to alter our perceptions of and responses to our fears and self-doubt. However, sometimes ignoring it is the best course of action. Give up worrying about what other people will think, about your own expectations, or even about the result in general, and just concentrate on completing one task at a time.

It might not seem like the most fun or straightforward course of action to choose to ignore fear, and it certainly isn't the simplest. We've adapted to recognise and acknowledge our fears and anxieties. What may have occurred if our forefathers had decided to put all of their attention on the stunning rock art they were producing and ignore their dread of the saber-toothed tiger over there? We wouldn't have had long to live as a species.

But fear often does more harm than good in today's environment. One effective way to keep going forward is to consciously decide to ignore that fear and concentrate on the work at hand.

Fear Of Failure's Effects On Personal And Professional Development: A perceived threat is what sets off the human sensation of fear. It is a fundamental survival mechanism that alerts our bodies to danger and triggers the fight-or-flight reaction. It is therefore crucial to keeping us safe.

On the other hand, those who constantly live in fear—whether from perceived threats or actual physical dangers—can suffer detrimental effects on all facets of their lives and possibly even lose their ability to function.

Fear readies us to respond to peril. Our body releases hormones in response to perceived threat that:

-Slow down or shut down systems that are not necessary for survival (like our digestive system) -Sharpen systems that could aid in survival (like vision). In order to run faster, our heart rate rises and blood supply to our muscles increases.

In order to assist us concentrate on the threat that is currently there and commit it to memory, our body also boosts the flow of hormones to the amygdala, a region of the brain. Our responses to fear influence the decisions we make in both our personal and professional lives.

Fear can appear even in the bravest of individuals. Fear has no regard for positions, histories, qualifications, or skill levels; it affects people at all levels of an organization.

The common performance-related worries listed below may have an impact on your own efficacy:

A dread of not succeeding: The fear of being or doing anything "wrong" is the dread of failure. Your underlying assumptions are that there is a "right" way to do things and that you are incapable of doing things in the correct way.

Horror of criticism: Making the most of personal success techniques is necessary to accept performance criticism as a gift rather than an attack. It is imperative that one develop oneself. Once a task or project is completed, ask for feedback. The more questions you have, the less fear you feel.

Apprehension About Assertiveness

I'm worried you'll become upset if I tell you what I think. I'm worried that you might be offended if I tell you how I really feel. I fear I'll lose my job if I inform you how your behavior towards me has a bad effect. Is there anything here that you recognise?

Respect for one another rather than fear is the foundation of assertiveness. I value your viewpoint just as much as mine when I share my opinions with you. By being honest with you and sharing my feelings about a work issue, I am fostering a relationship of trust. By describing how your behavior affected me negatively, I'm laying the groundwork for future interactions and setting expectations.

A lot of us are limiting our effectiveness by succumbing to these and other worries.

These coping strategies will help you overcome your habits and move on.

Put action first: Regardless of the outcome, take the one action you have been putting off. If things don't work out, that's alright. Maybe you'd like to reach out to someone who could support your company, but you're afraid of being turned down. It is irrelevant. Your objective is to act, not to concentrate on the result.

Change your wording: Speak positively instead of negatively. Make it a practice to speak positively to yourself. It's true that the "I think I can" mentality works!

Pretend to succeed until you do: Fake confidence when you're not sure. To project confidence on the outside, you don't always need to feel 100% confident within. Even if a lot of successful people are internally weak, what sets them apart is their willingness to keep going.

Discover new nonverbal cues: Your body acts as a breaker. Modify your usage of it. Take a few quiet moments in your workplace to relax and regain your composure if you notice yourself becoming tense. After that, proceed and deal with the issue or circumstance you are dealing with.

The effectiveness of most people is impacted by fear. If you can get the hang of it, you'll be able to achieve your goals both personally and professionally, putting you ahead of your peers!

Chapter Five: Success Is What You Make It.

A basic definition of success would be completing an objective that you had set out to complete in the past and arriving at a valuable or significant outcome for you or others.

Success is not an external result, but an interior transformation. It originates from facing your anxieties head-on and telling them to go away. And even if it might not be as immediately noticeable to others as money is, it is yct just as genuine. because it doesn't need tangible evidence and is straightforward and honest.

There are varying opinions regarding success; one such opinion is that it has ups and downs. that the secret to happiness is to face your anxieties. And defining it according to your own terms is necessary for true success. What keeps us always lacking is the necessity for a common concept of success. To truly succeed, you must value the aspects of yourself that set you apart from the crowd.

By defining success according to your own standards, you can live from knowledge and truth rather than the conventional one-size-fits-all strategy. Instead of running away from your talent because you believe success can only appear in particular ways, it enables you to embrace it. When tested, your concept of success will be flexible, authentic to you, and independent of other circumstances that have the power to make or break you. Your happiness won't be dependent on anything outside of yourself, so you won't be at the mercy of life's ups and downs. And isn't that, in the end, the main goal of success?

Nobody understands better than you what you want to achieve in life and what kind of success would mean the most to you.

The only person who truly understands your goals and what kind of success will provide you the most happiness, fulfillment, and significance in life is you.

Putting the answers to the following six questions down on paper is a quick and easy approach to define your own success:

What goals do I have for my life?

Why is it something I want to do?

When will I have it done?

Where am I going to do it?

How am I going to do that?

How will I be able to tell when I'm done?

After that, record your responses to each of the six questions on paper.

Your responses should only guide you in the direction of your desired outcome; they don't have to be flawless. Continue to review your definition of success frequently and make necessary adjustments.

The "why why" will motivate you to keep going as you map out a course, but the "how will I accomplish it" issue is the most difficult to answer up front. Your inner sense of direction will be provided by your ambition, drive, and internal compass.

No matter how long it takes or what obstacles you encounter along the road, find your motivation, your passion, your vision, your urge, and your reason for doing what you are doing. Then, embrace the will to keep going, learning, and persevering.

In what ways do you define success? Think carefully about your life goals for a while. It's simple to become engrossed in daily life's bustle and neglect to set aside time for ourselves. We lose sight of our own needs because we are preoccupied with making deadlines and completing tasks. However, we risk living someone else's dream rather than our own if we don't take the time to think about what it is that we really want out of life.

Thus, inhale deeply, unwind, and give yourself some space to consider your true desires. What brings you joy? What fervours do you have? Which kind of legacy are you hoping to leave? As soon as you are more clear about what you desire,

You can begin implementing little life adjustments that will support you in reaching your objectives after you have a clearer idea of what it is that you want.

Your idea of success ought to inspire and motivate you to begin and continue working on your path to success. Based on your concept of success, strive to be the best success you possibly can be. Aim for excellence in all that you do, and be aware of your motivations.

Being the greatest at something, including cooking, painting, gardening, singing, pursuing a job, acting, launching a business, teaching, swimming, writing, managing, leading, coding, designing, coaching, blogging, and being a good provider, are some examples of success.

Establish high expectations for your own accomplishments, excellence, and aspirations. Make use of your talents, skills, and abilities to further a goal you are dedicated to achieving.

The next action is to equip yourself with information and knowledge about the field in which you hope to succeed. Do some research and determine what steps you need to do to succeed.

Success in life shouldn't be limited to one particular endeavor; it can also involve pursuing and achieving a few goals in particular domains.

To succeed, picture yourself as a snowflake at the summit of a mountain, and your mission is to join forces with other snowflakes to roll down the mountain and eventually form an enormous force that will explode.

The key to success is finding that additional push in life. Success is a lifelong process where the objective is to constantly keep becoming better and better every day rather than a one-time or overnight activity or event. the next step is to advance as your new self in order to elevate and advance you in the direction of your life's goals.

Any series of deliberate actions or measures you take to better yourself can also be considered successful. The idea is to improve yourself from the inside out, meaning that you should become a better version of yourself now than you were yesterday, a year ago, or five years ago.

Increasing our impact on the people and environment around us is one of the key components of success.

Investing in your own development is one of the best investments you can make. Working on oneself, working with others, and working through others are the three ways that one might develop oneself. Nobody is independent; we all depend on one another.

Maintain a mental picture of your goals at all times, picture yourself achieving them, and consider yourself a success.

Success is achieving a predefined objective and completing a task that you set out to complete in the past and that is valuable or significant to you or others.

The only person who truly understands your goals and what kind of success will provide you the most happiness, fulfillment, and significance in life is you.

Success in life shouldn't be limited to one particular endeavor; it can also involve pursuing and achieving a few goals in particular domains.

Our purpose is to realize our own aspirations, not those of others. Humans are driven by the pursuit of happiness. Our desire for a brighter future propels us to conquer great challenges and bear extreme adversity. But what happens if, despite achieving our objective, we are not content? What if we feel stuck using our own standards for success?

Success comes to various people in different ways. Some people see wealth or power as a barometer for success. For some people, success is determined by their capacity to impact others. Others achieve it by merely discovering contentment and satisfaction in their daily lives. Hence, in the end, each person must define success for themselves.

It's simple to become engrossed in what other people view as success. You know, the luxurious home, the fancy car, the six-figure income. However, if you're not cautious, you could easily find yourself on a path that ends in disappointment and burnout.

That's why it's essential to define success according to your own standards. Find out what truly brings you joy and fulfillment. Perhaps it's pursuing a creative passion or spending more time with your family. You may start making decisions that are consistent with your values after you understand what is really important.

For if you don't, someone else will take care of it. Furthermore, it's highly unlikely that such a definition will coincide with your actual life goals. Regretfully, we may unintentionally feel pressured by the media, society, and even our loved ones to pursue achievement standards that are inconsistent with who we really are.

These are a few approaches to defining success elements that have proven effective for many people:

Create a board of goals: Making a vision board is an excellent method to inspire yourself and see your objectives clearly. Cut out photographs or pictures from publications that reflect your goals in life, and then glue them into a corkboard or poster. To help you remember your goals, post the board somewhere you'll see it every day, such as next to your computer monitor or on the wall of your bedroom.

Every day, set aside some time to contemplate. Even ten or fifteen minutes a day spent thinking about your objectives might add up over time. Write down your life goals, your reasons for wanting them, and the next steps you need to take to make them a reality at this period.

Sign up for a support group: Joining a support group of people who share your goals is a terrific approach to stay accountable and become motivated. This might be an online forum where individuals exchange ideas and tips or a group of friends who get together often to talk about their progress. To help you define your goals and determine how to get there, you can also work with mentors or coaches.

Tell yourself the truth about what brings you joy: It's simple to become engrossed in what we believe should bring us happiness. On social media, we see images of seemingly perfect individuals, and we start to think that if we had a few more things, we would too be content. However, the source of happiness is actually within. It has nothing to do with your possessions or your list of achievements. It all comes down to being frank about what brings you joy and figuring out how to surround yourself with more of those things.

Describe what success means to you in your own words: Recognise the end point you wish to pursue on your journey through life.

Continue to review your definition of success frequently and make necessary adjustments. Any series of deliberate efforts or steps you take to better yourself are considered successful.

Maintain a balanced biochemistry for lasting happiness: Whether we like it or not, chemicals have an impact on everything in our life. They influence our memories as well as our feelings and thoughts. It follows that their influence on happiness is not surprising. The four primary neurotransmitters that affect how happy we feel are serotonin, oxytocin, dopamine, and cortisol.

Because it is released in response to stress and can result in emotions of anxiety and irritation, cortisol is sometimes referred to as the "stress hormone." Your health will suffer if you are in a scenario that stresses you out all the time. By exercising, getting proper sleep, spending time in nature, and breathing gently, you can reduce it.

Because it is released when humans experience pleasure, dopamine is frequently referred to as the "feel good" chemical. Unfortunately, because it's so simple to obtain, the majority of us have unhealthy relationships with it. We get a temporary boost of happiness from fast food, booze, social media, binge-watching, and buying. To feel it again, though, we require more and more, much like junkies. Although dopamine helps us begin a challenging activity, it is not a sustainable source of motivation.

It has been demonstrated that oxytocin increases trust, lowers fear, and fosters wellbeing. In addition to improving mood and immune system strength, this potent hormone lowers stress levels and even speeds up the healing process from wounds. Creating strong emotional connections with those you love is the best approach to raise oxytocin. Not only does it make us feel good right then and there, but it also has long-term positive effects on our health and general well-being.

The "happy hormone" associated with contentment and relaxation is serotonin. Because it makes us feel good when we accomplish something meaningful, it is frequently referred to as the "accomplishment" chemical. To put it another way, serotonin is necessary for happiness. However, it's crucial to balance serotonin levels. An excessive emphasis on achievements may cause us to overlook important relationships in our lives, which lowers oxytocin levels.

Finding a balance between these two substances is necessary to experience true happiness.

Since our happiness is greatly influenced by all four of these chemicals, it is essential to recognise when they are present in our life. For the sake of you and your loved ones, you wish to lower cortisol. Utilise dopamine to get you started on difficult assignments and projects so that you can experience serotonin with each success and raise your intake of oxytocin by helping others and forming bonds with them.

While accumulating wealth may be a goal for some people, it's not always the only indicator of pleasure or success. Achieving one's own objectives, having a beneficial influence on others, or finding contentment in one's personal or professional life are just a few definitions of success.

It is crucial to remember that success and happiness are not always correlated with riches. Research has indicated that having more money does not always translate into being happier or having a more satisfying life after a certain point. Furthermore, chasing money at the price of other facets of life, like relationships or wellbeing, might have unfavorable effects.

Success is ultimately a subjective concept that can change depending on personal ideals and objectives. Prioritizing your personal fulfillment and significance in life is crucial, as opposed to concentrating only on material possessions or other external indicators of success.

Success is Defined on Your Own Terms: Why It Doesn't Matter What Others Think. It's important to define success according to your own criteria rather than fitting in with what other people think for a number of reasons.

1. Personal Fulfillment: You can pursue what truly fulfills you when you stick to your own definition of success, which will increase your level of happiness and contentment.

2. Distinctiveness: Rather than attempting to fit into a predetermined template, defining success for yourself recognises your distinctiveness and special strengths. Everybody's journey is different.

3. Lessened Stress: Breaking from society norms will help you feel less stressed and anxious because you won't be under pressure to live up to others' expectations.

4. Authenticity: Seeking your own brand of achievement promotes genuineness. Your life will have greater purpose if you stay loyal to who you are and what you believe in.

5. Innovation: Because you're not constrained by preconceived conceptions of what success should entail, deviating from the norm might inspire creative thinking and original solutions.

6. Resilience: Your drive is internal and not reliant on outside approval when you define success on your terms, which makes you more able to adjust to change and failures.

7. Self-Reflection: It promotes introspection, which aids in a better comprehension of your objectives, preferences, and moral principles.

In conclusion, defining success according to your own standards releases you from the confines of social norms and allows you to live a more real, personally meaningful, and rewarding life.

Many of us typically look to society for advice when determining success. We measure our own achievement against the accomplishments of others by taking a look at what others have accomplished. But it's crucial to keep in mind that success is a very subjective and individualized idea, so what one person may deem successful may not necessarily be the same for another.

As a result, it's essential to define success according to our own standards rather than letting society's expectations guide us.

Finding out what success means to each of us individually is one of the first steps towards creating our own definition of success. It's essential to consider our values, objectives, and aspirations in order to ascertain what matters most to us. Achieving financial stability may be the measure of success for some people, while having a rewarding work or a good family life may be the measure for others. We should make an effort to define success according to our own standards, regardless of what matters most to us.

Furthermore, it's essential to keep in mind that success is a relative concept. What makes one person happy might not make another happy, and what works for one person might not work for another. Our goal should be to define success according to our own standards, one that satisfies our needs and offers us genuine enjoyment.

After defining success for ourselves, we ought to concentrate on acting in a way that fulfils that criteria. This could entail following a certain professional route, creating deep connections, or devoting time and resources to one's own personal development. Whatever we decide to do, we should do it with purpose and intention rather than just because that's what society says we should do.

Living a purposeful and genuine life is greatly enhanced by taking ownership of our own definition of success. It enables us to turn our attention from outside influences or social norms to what really important to us.

"How do I go about realizing it?" is a question that arises once you know what you want out of life. Even though they have lofty goals, many people choose to lead average lives. The enormity of the work at hand may have overwhelmed them, or they may have given up on their own chances of success. How can you go from having dreams to acting upon them?

Setting Goals Is Essential for Determining Your Success

An objective is something we want to accomplish by taking action towards. Although the idea is rather straightforward, there are numerous ways to define the objectives. As an illustration, there are goals for each day, week, month, quarter, and year.

Simply said, there are major and minor objectives. We create goals in order to give our lives direction and meaning. Our lives can seem meaningless without them. We guarantee ourselves a certain amount of drive and ambition every day when we set goals.

Large Objectives (quarterly, monthly, and annual): These are goals that will take a lot of time to complete. These objectives frequently center on areas like money, health, house ownership, finding a new career, starting a relationship, etc. Put differently, the major objectives are focused on results.

You see, they are goals that need to be established. However, the lofty objectives by themselves won't aid in achieving them. The second category—small goals—is what leads to the accomplishment of the desired result.

Small Objectives (weekly & daily): In minor goals, the details matter a lot. Small goals must be created with the intention of accomplishing the larger goal once the larger goal has been established. They are seen as process goals as a result.

A process is the sequence of actions followed to accomplish a goal. Setting and meeting daily and weekly goals helps to keep us focused and responsible. When a well-thought-out plan is in place, the smaller objectives will take care of the bigger one. The best part is that there is no need for further worry. You will undoubtedly achieve your desired results if you have faith in the process and see through each of your tiny objectives.

You see, there's a lot more likelihood of success when a big goal is broken down into smaller ones. For this reason, having both big and little goals is crucial since they complement one another.

Establishing goals is essential to determining your level of achievement. It offers guidance, inspiration, and an obvious route to the achievement you want. Here's why creating goals is crucial:

1. Clarity: Whether in your personal, professional, or other endeavours, goals assist you in defining your objectives. They translate vague aspirations into concrete, quantifiable goals.

2. Motivation: Having goals gives you a reason to live. Having specific goals to strive for increases the likelihood of maintaining dedication and concentration.

3. Measurability: Specific objectives can be quantified. This enables you to monitor your advancement and evaluate if you're getting nearer to your ideal of success.

4. Accountability: You are responsible to yourself when you set goals. It's a means to make sure you're moving in the right direction towards your own definition of success.

5. Adaptability: As conditions change or you come to new realizations about what success means to you, you can modify your goals. They allow you to be flexible in your search.

6. Prioritization: Setting goals aids in the order of duties and pursuits. Your time and resources can be used more wisely if they are in line with your goals.

7. Achievement: Reaching objectives increases self-esteem and gives you a sense of accomplishment, which adds to your overall success.

8. Long-Term Vision: Setting goals, whether short- or long-term, will help you make a plan for your

success in the future and make sure you're aiming for the right things.

Keep in mind that your objectives should match your own notion of success rather than just what society considers to be successful. You may define and attain success on your own terms and live a more purposeful and satisfying life by setting goals that are significant to you.

Goal-Setting's Significance

Why are goals even necessary in the first place? Since nothing in life should be done unless there is a compelling reason to do so, that is a good question that deserves an answer.

The direction and purpose that objectives offer are what give them worth. We give ourselves something to aim for when we make goals. Maintaining that final outcome makes life more organised and meaningful.

Setting goals fosters a lot of positive traits. Motivation is required to work towards a goal every day once it has been established. It's also necessary to practise focus.

Giving ourselves objectives to strive towards makes each day more purposeful and effective. Making a plan is hard without a defined objective. And we probably won't be as productive if we don't have a plan.

A goal can be anything!

One of the most lovely things about goal setting is this. It's a common misconception that a goal needs to be big in order to be set, but that is untrue. Setting goals is something we can do in any area of our lives.

Setting and achieving goals increases our chances of success significantly. Since goal-setting produces structure, focus, and direction.

The importance is the same whether the goals are big or small, daily or weekly. It is more likely that we will succeed in life if we have a well-defined plan. It may also result in a life that is more satisfying.

Goal planning is therefore very valuable, and the advantages that come from it are similarly remarkable.

Goal-Setting's Advantages

We now understand the purpose of goal setting and its benefits. However, what about the advantages that come with the practise?

There are numerous advantages that follow goal-setting. Among them are the following:

Boosts Inspiration: We are more motivated in two ways when we have goals. They first provide us with an objective to strive for. Having a goal gives us a certain amount of drive to accomplish it.

Secondly, our motivation increases with every goal we achieve, no matter how big or small. This is because reaching a goal makes us feel proud of ourselves, which inspires us to keep going.

Gives One a Feeling of Accountability: Assuming personal accountability for our lives is crucial to our prosperity and general well-being. We give ourselves something to strive for when we set goals. We have created the objective, so we will be the ones to achieve it."

Enables Progress Tracking: This is particularly valid for more modest objectives. In my experience, if I only establish a lofty goal, I frequently end up giving up because I am discouraged along the road. This occurs because it is difficult to recognise all of the tiny advancements achieved along the route.

We can keep track of all the work we've completed by creating little goals. Even if it's a concern.

Makes You Establish Priorities: Setting priorities is essential if we are to achieve anything in life. To avoid becoming sidetracked, you need to establish priorities for yourself. Goal-setting is a great way to help with that.

There are some priorities that emerge when we set big goals, followed by lesser ones.

Objectives that we hope to accomplish through activity are called goals. These goals provide our lives direction, clarity, focus, and meaning.

Along with daily and weekly goals, we can also create ambitious ones. Increasing motivation, developing a stronger feeling of accountability, monitoring progress, and aiding in the establishment of priorities are some advantages of this practise.

Chapter Six: Mentoring and Guidance

Fundamentally, mentorship is a partnership between two people in which one (the mentor) imparts knowledge, skills, and experience to another (the mentee). To assist the mentee develop and accomplish their objectives, the mentor offers direction, encouragement, and feedback. There are many different ways to mentor someone, ranging from unstructured one-on-one interactions to more organised programmes offered by organisations.

Both mentors and their mentees can gain a great deal from mentoring. Building this relationship can benefit your career development, networking, and ability to learn new things. Knowing these advantages can assist you in choosing whether to look for or accept a mentor.

A mentor is a person who provides guidance to a less experienced person, also referred to as their mentee. People usually look for mentors who are in their preferred field or the same field as them. The mentor assists the protégé in advancing and maturing as a professional, frequently providing guidance grounded in their broader expertise or experience. Formal mentorship programmes, personal contacts, and networking can all be used to establish mentoring relationships. Everyone benefits from mentoring.

Skill Development: Mentoring enables people to enhance and acquire new talents. In order to help mentees learn from both their achievements and failures, mentors offer advice on particular jobs or projects as well as sharing personal experiences.

Career Advancement: By giving mentees insightful knowledge about their business or profession, mentorship helps mentees progress their careers.

Mentors provide guidance on professional growth, networking, and employment prospects.

Personal Development: Mentoring promotes personal development in people. Mentors assist mentees in identifying their talents and limitations, provide emotional support and direction, and motivate them to take on new tasks.

Mentoring fosters a sense of community and connection inside the workplace, which raises employee engagement and retention.

The benefits of having a mentor include: 1. Mentors encourage progress: A mentor supports and facilitates the career or personal growth of their protégé. A mentor who sets goals and provides feedback can assist in helping them stay focused. Thus, businesses that wish to develop the abilities of their staff members frequently establish mentorship programmes. The expertise of the mentors can aid in educating and developing a talented and effective workforce. Workplaces that foster growth are valued by employees because it shows them that their employer respects them and wants to see them succeed.

2. Mentors facilitate relationships: A mentor can assist their mentee in expanding their professional network. The mentor can help the mentee find chances or people who can support them when they identify their goals, whether they be professional or personal. These relationships can be helpful for job progression because the mentor usually has more industry experience or a higher-level career.

3. Mentors can aid in goal-setting: A mentor can assist their mentee in establishing goals for their career or personal growth. They can make SMART goals—specific, attainable, relevant, and time-based—for efficient goal-setting. These objectives can aid in the mentee's concentration and facilitate the mentor's ability to monitor and evaluate development. They might choose to focus

on minor projects in order to achieve a bigger goal,
such as meeting deadlines or honing a certain set of
abilities.

4. Mentors are a source of information: The
mentee's success can be facilitated by the
specialized knowledge and insights that mentors
can offer. For instance, they provide guidance on
how to carry out specific duties or acquire beneficial
abilities. People just starting out in their careers can
gain from this kind of advice since it makes them
more at ease in their roles more rapidly. A mentor,
for instance, can assist someone launching a firm in
learning how to create their first budget and
business plan.

5. Mentors provide support: The mentee can seek
assistance from their mentor if they are having
trouble doing their work or accomplishing a goal.
This support can inspire individuals to keep going
in spite of obstacles. In order to provide their
mentee confidence, a mentor might also recognise

and highlight their abilities. A strong sense of confidence might help the mentee stay motivated to pursue their objectives.

6. Mentors uphold responsibility: When it comes to their objectives, a mentor holds their mentee accountable. The mentor assists the mentee in maintaining concentration and staying on pace to finish them by monitoring progress. Additionally, it can guarantee that the mentee remembers the objectives they have set. The mentee may be more motivated if they are aware that others are observing, since they are probably reluctant to disappoint their mentor by not achieving their objectives.

7. Mentors act as dependable allies: A fundamental component of mentoring partnerships is trust. The mentee needs to have faith that the mentor will provide them accurate and truthful advice, and that they will act in their best interests. Because the corporate sector can be competitive, they must rely

on one another to protect sensitive information
when needed. Two strategies for building trust in
these situations are to communicate frequently and
to keep their word.

8. Mentors are able to provide helpful criticism:
Honest feedback is made possible by a mentorship
relationship based on trust. By developing a
relationship of trust, the mentee comes to realize
that constructive criticism is meant to advance their
career development rather than cause them
distress. Mentors can help students improve by
pointing out their areas of weakness. Because of the
professional nature of the connection, the mentor
assumes an impartial role. In the meantime, a
friend might be reluctant to point out the mentee's
shortcomings out of concern that they would come
out as judgmental.

9. Mentors are receptive to hearing: When someone
has an idea, they might discuss or attempt it with a
mentor as a resource. The mentor's relevant

knowledge and experience can be used to offer objective advise or opinions. The mentee will be better able to decide what actions to take and whether to pursue the idea or not after receiving these insights. In a similar vein, a mentor can also listen to them and offer guidance on day-to-day issues like disagreements at work.

10. Mentors possess pertinent expertise: People should, if at all possible, select mentors with appropriate experience for their goals or line of work. When mentors share their accomplishments, mentees might take inspiration from them and emulate the actions they took. Mentors might also discuss the errors they made on their path. The mentee gains because they do not have to bear the consequences of their mistakes; instead, they acquire lessons about their harmful effects. Knowing about these experiences can also help the mentee get ready for impending obstacles and offer concrete guidance on how to get past them.

11. A free resource are mentors: Mentors don't usually ask for compensation; instead, it usually happens as a result of workplace programmes or networking. They volunteer to take on this position out of a genuine desire to support the other person's development and forge a closer, more real bond. Additionally, by not charging for mentorship, it becomes available to a wider range of individuals as opposed to only those with the means to do so.

12. Mentors offer advice: For those who are just beginning their career, a mentor can assist in establishing expectations for the workplace. For instance, they might make clear the importance of the position and acceptable workplace conduct. These recommendations can assist the mentee in developing productive work habits that will help them concentrate and do their jobs well. They can be more productive and make an impression on their managers with these productive work practises.

The secret to establishing and maintaining a fulfilling professional career is mentoring. Through mentoring, we may all develop, learn, change, and achieve our goals in fundamental, clinical, and translational research as well as in education. Whether you are a world-class investigator, a senior educator, or you are just starting your professional training, mentoring ensures that each person succeeds in achieving their personal and professional career goals while also contributing to the development of a vibrant community.

Having a mentor can make all the difference in the complicated and frequently fiercely competitive world of academic medicine today. Mentoring can help to guarantee a successful conclusion, whether you're looking for guidance on how to formulate a research topic, how to best design a new experiment, how to team-teach a course, or where to discover all the necessary materials. A mentor can guarantee consistent progress and the accomplishment of project milestones by taking on the role of a guide, coach, or ally and responding to questions as they come up for the mentee. A mentor who takes on the role of an advocate can assist a mentee in navigating the academic landscape and advancing in their career.

A mentor's attention and encouragement can provide a mentee the courage to take on a novel and stimulating project.

When it comes to assisting people in overcoming failure, mentors and guides are invaluable. In spite of failures, they support both professional and personal growth in the following ways:

1. Emotional Support: This is a vital resource in times of failure. Mentors and guides can help people deal with disappointment and frustration by providing support, empathy, and a listening ear.

2. Learning from Mistakes: Mentors assist people in reflecting on their setbacks and helping them draw conclusions and lessons that can result in both professional and personal development.

3. Advice: Mentors provide advice on how to get over challenges, build resilience, and deal with failures. They might offer helpful guidance and problem-solving techniques.

4. Networking: People can access a mentor's network of contacts and resources, which can be especially helpful when attempting to move past a setback.

5. Perspective: Drawing from their own experiences, mentors offer insightful viewpoints. They can help people understand the wider picture by providing insight into how mistakes are frequently stepping stones to achievement.

6. Confidence-Building: A skilled mentor can help someone regain their self-assurance by pointing out their abilities and strengths, especially in the face of setbacks.

7. Promoting Persistence: Mentors can inspire people to keep trying after a setback by stressing how important resilience and tenacity are to long-term success.

8. Accountability: In order to move on after a setback, mentors can assist people in setting new objectives and holding them responsible for their accomplishments.

In conclusion, mentors and guides may be very helpful in helping people not only accept failure as a necessary part of life but also to use it as a springboard for future success. They provide a blend of wisdom, practical guidance, and emotional support. In the face of obstacles, they offer a crucial lifeline for both professional and personal development.

Mentors assist and encourage others to advance in their lives and careers. In order to assist the mentee in reaching their objectives, they offer guidance and comments while sharing their expertise and experiences.

A mentor is similar to a reliable friend and counselor; they provide frank and compassionate dialogues to illuminate fresh possibilities and surmount obstacles. The mentee can benefit from this relationship in many ways, including increased confidence, improved problem-solving skills, and wider networks. It is essential for professional development.

With the aid of the mentor's knowledge and experience, the mentee aims to advance both personally and professionally. Through the mentor's guidance, the mentee's abilities, self-assurance, and career prospects are to be enhanced in the mentor-mentee relationship.

Famous Mentors and Mentees: Examples

Mark Zuckerberg and Steve Jobs: In the early stages of Facebook, Mark Zuckerberg received mentorship from Steve Jobs, who gave him counsel and direction. Jobs gave insightful advice on staying focused and getting back to the company's core goals. The mentorship helped Zuckerberg succeed by having a long-lasting effect on Facebook and Zuckerberg.

Steve Warren and Bill Gates: Though first reluctant, Warren Buffett and Bill Gates forged a mentor-mentee relationship. Buffett posed insightful questions to Gates, which caused him to reconsider his views on philanthropy and corporate management. Gates said that Buffett taught him how to prioritize people and manage his time well, which changed the way he approached many areas of his life.

Being a mentee is a chance for development and education that necessitates proactive participation and receptivity to fresh viewpoints. To progress in both your personal and professional development, be open and honest with your mentor, accept challenges, and take calculated chances.

Communicate proactively with your mentor by sharing your objectives and interests as well as by asking questions.

Give your mentor your full attention and reply to their messages or requests right away.

Be clear about your needs and let your mentor know how they can help you most.

Recognise that while your mentor can provide support and direction, they cannot resolve every issue you may have.

During mentorship sessions, pay attention and think about how you might use the input to better yourself.

Future leaders need the knowledge and direction that mentors provide. Their influence is significant, increasing self-esteem and broadening ties. Embracing the power of mentorship can unlock true potential and lead to an exciting future filled with possibilities. Whether seeking guidance or aspiring to become a mentor, understanding the importance of mentors and the transformative experiences they provide can ignite a powerful journey of personal growth and success. The future is full of opportunities and limitless promise when you have mentors at your side. So go forth and seize the amazing benefits that mentors can bring to your life!

How Mentorship Can Offer Vital Assistance During Difficult Times

Mentorship can provide vital assistance during trying times, particularly when one is confronting failure. Here's how mentoring may offer this essential assistance:

1. Emotional Support: During difficult times, mentors can lend a sympathetic and understanding ear, providing the emotional support that is frequently required. They can lessen feelings of loneliness, assist people in processing their emotions, and give them hope again.

2. Viewpoint: Having seen their fair share of setbacks, mentors frequently possess a more comprehensive outlook. They may shed light on how setbacks are a necessary component of all journeys and present chances for development.

3. Gaining Knowledge from Experience: Mentors assist individuals in drawing insightful conclusions from their setbacks by sharing their own experiences, even their mistakes. Individuals can prevent making the same mistakes by using this knowledge.

4. Reevaluating and refining goals: Mentors can help people develop reasonable and attainable goals by assisting in goal evaluation and refining. The demotivation that frequently follows failure can be overcome in large part through this method.

5. Mentors offer support and inspiration by serving as a constant reminder of a person's abilities, potential, and qualities. Rebuilding resilience and confidence after a setback can be facilitated by this.

6. Accountability and Guidance: By providing direction and keeping people accountable for their actions and advancement, mentors assist people in establishing a road towards recovery.

7. Networking and Resources: After a loss, mentors
may help people get back on track by introducing
them to opportunity, resources, and useful contacts.

8. Long-Term Perspective: By highlighting that
success is still possible in the long run, mentors
assist people in viewing failure as a temporary
setback as opposed to a permanent condition.

9. Fostering Resilience: As people learn how to
overcome obstacles, adjust, and carry on,
mentoring can help people become more resilient.

In conclusion, mentorship offers a special blend of
psychological, practical, and inspirational
assistance that is priceless in trying circumstances,
like accepting defeat. The wisdom and experience of
a mentor can help people face failure head-on with
more fortitude and tenacity, which eventually
results in progress on both a personal and
professional level.

Conclusion

"Failure as a Path to Success: Embracing Setbacks As Learning Opportunities" offers a thorough examination of the transformational potential of setbacks and the priceless lessons they may teach on the path to both professional and personal development. This book offers a new perspective on the often-overlooked bright spots hidden within failures, making it a beacon of hope for anybody who has faced setbacks and disappointments in their quest for achievement.

With the help of his own experiences and observations, as well as his elegant and approachable writing style, Drew S. Baldridge crafts a story that will captivate readers of various backgrounds. He breaks down the stigma associated with failure and reframes it as a necessary step on the path to realizing one's goals.

By emphasizing the personal accounts of individuals.

He breaks down the stigma associated with failure and reframes it as a necessary step on the path to realizing one's goals. Drew shows how everyone has the capacity for greatness by presenting the tales of people who have triumphed over adversity.

This book offers helpful advice on using setbacks as effective tools for self-improvement in addition to encouraging readers to accept and even welcome them. It encourages a mental change from one of fearing failure to actively seeking it out as a way to advance one's career and personal growth.

Drew's work serves as evidence for the theory that our biggest successes frequently result from our biggest failures. By stressing that failure is not an end but rather a beginning and an essential step on the path to achievement, it challenges the current quo. After reading this book, readers will feel immensely empowered since they now know that they can overcome hardship and turn it to their benefit.

It is our aim that when the last page of this book is turned, readers will have the knowledge, fortitude, and steadfast resolve to take on life's obstacles head-on. It's a life-changing manual that helps people accept responsibility for their mistakes. Drew S. Baldridge's "Failure as a Path to Success" is more than just a book; it's a transformative guide that enables people to embrace their own potential, harness their setbacks, and forge a path towards both personal and professional triumph.

This book serves as a reminder that success frequently rises from the ashes of our failures and is a monument to the human spirit's amazing capacity for growth and resilience.